The Enemies of Excellence

Enemy One: Egotism.

"I know best."

Enemy Two: Life Mismanagement.

"I'll get to it later."

Enemy Three: Bad Habits.

"What harm could it do?"

Enemy Four: Indulgence.

"I just can't help myself"

Enemy Five: Broken Relationships.

"I don't really need people."

Enemy Six: Isolation.

"I can do it on my own."

Enemy Seven: Self-sabotage.

"It's not my fault."

the enemies of excellence

7 reasons why we sabotage success

GREG SALCICCIOLI

CROSSROAD NEW YORK

The Crossroad Publishing Company
www.CrossroadPublishing.com

In continuation of our 200-year tradition of independent publishing, The Crossroad Publishing Company proudly offers a variety of books with strong, original voices and diverse perspectives. The viewpoints expressed in our books are not necessarily those of The Crossroad Publishing Company, any of its imprints or of its employees. No claims are made or responsibility assumed for any health or other benefit.

Printed in the United States of America.
The text of this book is set in Apollo.
The display face is Verdana.

Project Management by
The Crossroad Publishing Company
John Jones

For this edition numerous people have shared their talents and ideas, and we gratefully acknowledge Greg Salciccioli, who has been most gracious during the course of our cooperation. We thank especially:

| Cover design: Faceout Studio | Text design: Scribe |
| Proofreading: Sylke Jackson | Printing: Versa Press |

Message development, text development, package, and market positioning by
The Crossroad Publishing Company

Cataloging-in-Publication Data is available from the Library of Congress

Books published by The Crossroad Publishing Company may be purchased at special quantity discount rates for classes and institutional use. For information, please e-mail info@CrossroadPublishing.com

ISBN 13: 978-0-8245-2626-9

14 13 12 11

Table of Contents

Acknowledgments

This book is the result of a team effort. Many extraordinary people have contributed to not only the writing of this resource but my education and experience. I would like to acknowledge these incredibly gifted people.

First, I want to thank Matthew Kelly for his friendship, encouragement, and introduction to the Crossroad Publishing team: from Gwendolin Herder, the gracious CEO of Crossroad who believed in me and this book, to Dr. John Jones, the Editorial Director who provided sage advice and expert editing. Without John, *The Enemies of Excellence* would never have reached its full potential and become the valuable resource it is today. He is a gifted writer and has become a good friend. Patrick Lencioni and the Table Group team are experts in the field of leadership and management. I greatly appreciate their friendship, encouragement, and excellent guidance. Their contributions brought clarity and depth to this resource. A special thanks to my great friends Daniel Harkavy and Michael Van Skaik for their coaching and constant encouragement. I also want to thank my research assistant Lauren Ruef for investing countless hours in building the book's foundation, as well as Dan and Fran Berrey for helping fund the project.

Next, I offer my sincere gratitude to my colleagues at Building Champions and Ministry Coaching International. Without your support, ideas, and passion, this book would not have been written. All of you are gifted professionals who have dedicated your lives to improving the lives of leaders around the world.

A special thanks to the leaders I have had the honor of coaching and consulting in the last decade. Your passion to pursue excellence is a constant encouragement in my life.

I want to thank Dianna, my best friend and bride as well as my amazing family, for your constant support. Each of you brings tremendous joy to my life, and I am very thankful for each of you.

Finally I give thanks to God the Father, the Son, and the Holy Spirit for all that I am.

Foreword by Patrick Lencioni

Whenever a high profile leader or personality falls from grace—because of drugs, alcohol, infidelity, financial mismanagement or another similar malady—it's not easy to find sympathy among the general public. After all, these are famous, wealthy people we're talking about, and they seem to bring on their own misery through the decisions they make. If anything, people take delight in seeing them learn painful lessons in humility.

Of course, this callousness toward high profile misery is misguided for a whole host of reasons, the most obvious of which is the collateral suffering that is inevitably mixed in with the carnage. Innocent spouses, children, friends, and employees are affected in profound ways, and even shareholders, customers, and fans can experience very real suffering as a result of a leader's destruction.

Well, as it turns out, there is another reason to feel bad when leaders set fire to their careers and their lives—those leaders are probably victims of an insidiously destructive and predictable pattern of behavior that plagues even some of the most well-intentioned people. According to Greg Salciccioli, and his theory makes a lot of sense, there is something inherent in being a person of influence that creates a likelihood of pain and self-destruction.

Greg has seen this first-hand, again and again. As a coach to leaders, he's come to recognize the signs of impending tragedy, and the dangerous tendencies which propel a leader unknowingly toward despair and misery beyond their comprehension.

This book is a wake-up call for all people who find themselves in positions of leadership and influence, and who want to preserve their families, their organizations, their self-respect, and their peace of heart and mind. The tragedy that can be avoided by heeding the advice here, and the joy that can be experienced through authentic, humble leadership, makes this a treasure.

—Patrick Lencioni, president, The Table Group;
author, *The Five Dysfunctions of a Team*

Chapter One

Don't Play with Matches!

"Don't play with matches! You could hurt yourself and burn down the house." Sounds like good advice, but to a 10-year-old boy it doesn't mean much. He's thinking: "I got it, Mom and Dad. I can handle this. Nothing bad is going to happen to me."

I wish that was true.

It was the summer of 1970, and instead of playing in the sprinklers with my buddies, I found myself in the backyard doing my chore, picking up piles of weeds. Begrudgingly, I bagged the weeds and hauled them to the front sidewalk for trash day pick-up.

It's said that necessity is the mother of invention, and in my need to play with my friends as soon as possible, I had struck upon a brilliant idea. I could burn up the weeds, one pile at a time, and my chore would be completed much faster. With this notion in my mind, I snuck into the garage and grabbed a box of matches, returning to my boring task with a renewed sense of excitement. I began with great enthusiasm, arranging a small pile of weeds, striking a match and watching the pile burn. It worked great. Then I realized that if I increased the size of the piles, the task would get done much faster!

You can guess what happened next. I made an extra-large pile of dry weeds in the center of the yard, stood back, and threw a match onto the pile. At first the flame was so small I could barely see it, but then it grew into a raging ball of fire. They flames grew so large that the pile began to ignite the other piles close to it, and soon the entire backyard was up in flames. The rubber on the soles of my shoes was melting as I frantically stomped on the consuming fire while trying to douse the weeds with a garden hose. As hard as I tried, though, it was futile—the flames continued to advance at an alarming rate.

I will never forget the image of my poor mother screaming and waving her hands in the air as she looked through the window at her backyard engulfed in flames.

Fortunately, mom called for help. I could hear the sirens, then see the men rushing to save me from my futile fire-fight. The firemen pulled up in front of our house, stretched their fire hoses into the backyard, and put out the fire before it spread to our house and the neighbors' houses. I was escorted onto the street by a particularly stern fireman and commanded to stay inside the fire engine until things were under control.

That night as I rubbed my backside, still sore from a well-deserved spanking, I reflected on how quickly the situation got out of control. I was amazed at how fast my good intentions turned into a raging fire. Despite my parents' warnings, I really thought I could manage the fire, when in reality I was playing with a force much more powerful and destructive than I knew.

Fortunately, except for some ruined sneakers, nothing serious happened that day, but sometimes in life the house really does catch fire and burn to the ground.

A Firestorm in the Front Room

Rob was an exceptional leader who had everything going for him. He was smart, an amazing communicator and motivator. In a short amount of time, he had built a successful organization. People loved to follow him. So did I.

I will never forget the day he called for help.

The call came early and shattered the silence. I did my best to ignore the obnoxious ringing, but it just wouldn't work. I wrestled myself out of bed and made the long walk to the phone in the kitchen. At that moment I just wanted to be in that place of retreat and restoration. I wanted my sleep!

I answered the phone. Rob had never called me before at such an early hour, and his voice was troubled.

"Greg, I need your help. Can you please come to my house?" It was less of a question than a statement.

"Rob, what's wrong?"

"I'll explain when you get here—it's too hard to explain over the phone."

"Give me 30 minutes."

I jumped in the shower to wake up and take a few minutes to sort out the many thoughts that were filling my mind. I had known Rob for more than a decade and mentored him in his life and leadership. I hired him to work with me in a former organization. He was a friend I respected and cared deeply for. He was a gifted leader with amazing potential, a highly driven individual with endless energy. But there were problems. I knew that he tended to work too many hours. As I flashed back to recent conversations, I recalled seeing turmoil and anxiety in his heart. He'd been unfocused and excessively emotional. He looked like he could melt down at any moment. His wife didn't support his overworked and under-nourished lifestyle, and this produced a steady stream of stress and tension in their home life. Was Rob's wife concerned for his work-induced weariness? Could this be the problem?

No, it must be something different. Rob was also was known as a maverick, someone who did not like to follow rules and avoided close accountability. He always seemed to be pushing the limits and liked the fact that he could counter conventional leadership methods and manipulate situations to control their outcomes. He'd been warned that he was going too far, but every warning only seemed to make him bolder. Had he made a rash leadership move that created a mess? Or was it something else?

As I dressed and prepared to leave, I hoped it was not a serious problem, but I felt a growing sense of concern and anxiety as my bride caught my eyes on my way out the door. We both knew there was trouble. How could we help?

I pulled onto Rob's street and parked to sit in silence. I needed to pray and prepare for the worst. I didn't know what I would learn, but I could tell it would be tragic. It needed great wisdom, care, and a proper course of action. Already at that time, I had worked with great leaders who had fallen. It was always the same familiar patterns and the same predictably tragic ending. They played with matches one too many times. But not this time. Lord, no, please. Not this time.

As I approached the driveway, I wondered what fires Rob had been playing with that I didn't even know about. What heart issues, decisions, and actions collided to create this crisis? Who was involved and what would this mean to Rob, his family, friends, associates, and to his role as a leader?

Even though I'd done my best to gather my thoughts in the short time I had, nothing could have prepared me for what I was about to witness. Some events in life defy understanding and description. This was one. As I reached the front door, the quiet of the morning was upset by screaming and weeping. Behind that door a tragic event was unfolding. A life was coming undone—maybe more than one.

Rob opened the door and looked like he had been on a battlefield. A trail of fingernail scratches covered his face. His eyes showed horror, confusion, fatigue, and fear. Before I could respond, he motioned to the family room, where the sound of agonized weeping came from.

I walked slowly down the hallway toward the family room, reluctant to witness someone in such severe distress. As I entered the room another scream pierced my soul. It carried an intensity that forever changed me. It was Rob's wife. Her cries expressed the anger of deception; she had been betrayed. Her sanity and security were shattered. Their marital fidelity had been forever violated by the very person who had vowed to protect it. I listened while she shared the details of her husband's affair. His house was on fire, and it was burning to the ground.

The fire had not finished its destruction. I quickly thought of Rob's children and hoped they were not present to witness the pillars of their home in such emotional disarray.

My heart was heavy and burdened with this perplexing reality. What could be done? Should Rob and his wife be separated to calm the situation? Was now the time to confront Rob and try to lead the couple to some point of reconciliation? I sat there stunned for quite a while as I filtered these thoughts, fighting to keep composure and listen for as long as I could stand.

As I looked around the room, I began to survey the damage in the lives around me. A colleague had joined us, bringing with him a friend with medical training to soothe Rob's wife. She was able to provide the much needed comfort we could not. After his wife departed, we were left to face our own raw emotions. We sat there for a long time—just looking at Rob. On this ordinary Monday morning, we should all be at work, serving people and meeting the demands of our weekly workload. Instead, we were at the epicenter of a heart-wrenching firestorm that would alter the course of Rob's life, his children, his staff, and everyone employed by the organization he led.

The colleague and I were appalled at Rob's adultery. We were overrun with anger and bitter feelings of being duped. We had trusted Rob and given him our full support. We had labored alongside him to build a great organization and expected that he would reciprocate with moral and ethical character. Our trust had been shattered and lost in the secrecy of his life. He had played us for fools.

Why Leaders Sabotage Their Own Success

Failed leadership is an issue in all parts of our culture. We see it in the headlines with a frequency unheard of in the past. It is easy for us to think that the problem resides in *other people's* lives, their money, their fame, and their power. But the struggles that high profile leaders face are in many ways identical to the ones you and I face every day, in our offices, homes, and schools. This has become clear to me in my 25 years of working with people—the same pattern occurs over and over again. It is everywhere. You probably know someone who has crashed and burned. Like me, you have been compelled to ask "why?" Why do talented, bright people with great potential and influence destroy their lives and damage those who love and support them? How do these catastrophes happen to people who have everything going for them and their families? Is there anything they can do to prevent it? And is there anything *we* can do to prevent it? The answer is yes—first of all by:

- recognizing the hazards intrinsic to all forms of leadership,
- realizing that we are just as vulnerable as the most famous and illustrious of high-profile leaders, and
- taking the steps in this book to pull ourselves away from the fire.

Why do leaders, even the greatest of them, sabotage their own success? No one has said it better than a good friend and fellow colleague, Dr. Wayde Goodall, in his book *Why Great Men Fall*:

> There are reasons people make bad choices, and it doesn't happen overnight. There is an evolution—one thought, decision, or a move at a time. They decided to go to the wrong place, ask the wrong question, look at illegal or immoral materials, or have a conversation with someone they knew was compromising. The behavior began somewhere. I don't believe this kind of "life altering" failure just hits like a brick on some particular day. There is a process—sometimes it can be short lived—sometimes it works on a person for years. Some call it temptation; others call it a hazard of success.[1]

In my coaching, I have found this to be true. *It doesn't happen overnight.* The house does not burn down the first time you play with matches. There are always warning signs. As leaders, unfortunately, we are often moving too fast to notice the signs. Maybe you don't cheat on your spouse, but you fall into other traps. You push yourself too hard. You congratulate yourself with words like "I built this company with my own two hands," becoming arrogant and dangerous. You decide that the rules don't apply to you. You tell yourself "I just don't have time for a personal life." Every leader faces risks in his role, and the greater the success, the greater the risk.

The bad news is that these traps, these Enemies of Excellence, are everywhere. I've seen these Enemies at work in the lives of people from CEOs to managers, staff members, and clients and customers. They can affect anyone, and they can affect you, no matter how successful you are, and no matter whether the last story written about you was in the *Wall Street Journal* or your spouse's Facebook page.

Here's the good news. By learning to recognize the Enemies of Excellence, you can conquer them before they conquer you, regardless of the kind of leadership role you play in life. I promise you this. For years I have been training and coaching leaders to recognize the risks in their lives and learn how to prevent a crisis before it arises. Through the stories in this book, we'll remind ourselves of many of the high-profile leadership disasters that have appeared in the headlines, both recent and historical, as well as considering examples from everyday life (including my own). At each stage of the journey, we'll also trace Rob's story backwards, to see how he came to the terrible place we saw earlier, and forward, to discover how he learned to turn his life around and regain his ability as a leader.

Chapter Two

Why We Sabotage Our Success

Why do successful people sabotage their own success?

This question troubled me for a long time. It seemed to defy an answer. Why would anyone work so hard to be successful and then, against all sound judgment, throw it away with ridiculous behavior? You would think that if someone invested so much energy in becoming successful, they would invest just a little more energy to ensure that their success would be sustainable. Logically, this makes sense, but it overlooks a key point. *Few people consider how to sustain their success because they're too busy trying to achieve it.*

Let me share with you how I came to a clearer understanding of this fascinating, disturbing phenomenon and its solution.

I'm a professional coach. Even my most boring day is filled with new insights. I'm called to come alongside some of the most amazing people on this planet. It's a job that fits me well. I care for each person I have the privilege to coach. I join people in their lives and leadership journeys. I become aware of their challenges and opportunities in real time, and together we tackle key issues and discover solutions that lead to results. Personal coaching provides a safe secure environment that allows evaluation and introspection to take place. It's amazing the clarity you can gain when two people are addressing life and leadership issues.

My own coaching style is to ask probing questions that help people think better and understand how to drive to solutions. The more questions I asked, the more humbled I became at the dedication I saw in so many people. Most leaders want to be the best people they can be and to lead with excellence. They want to thrive, and they want the people around them to thrive. They have the best of intentions.

At the same time, they find themselves in precarious positions. They are building successful organizations, but their health and personal lives don't get the same care they once did. Over the years, it can get worse and worse. There just doesn't seem to be time to do both well. This competition for time comes up in our coaching. Leaders ask: "I can't just ignore my professional responsibilities, but how do I keep going without self-destructing? How can I build a better personal life?" They recognize the problem but not how to address it.

In this case, "they" is potentially "each one of us." What I've found in my work is that most of us don't understand what it takes to build sustainable success, so we end up being our own saboteur. Success is inherently unstable. The skills it took to establish success cannot sustain it.

In my work with hundreds of leaders over the last decade, I've discovered several reasons we sabotage our own success. Some hazards are inherent in leadership and success, and the situation with high-profile leaders is even more hazardous. Leaders are not fully aware of the hazards, however—usually because no one told them to look for them (they lacked a personal coach or other trusted advisor), and leaders don't have the luxury of taking the time to figure them out on their own. Of course, people can't avoid what they don't see, so leaders don't have a plan for avoiding the hazards. In such a situation, failure is inevitable, sooner or later.

Arrogance

As I worked with and listened to hundreds of clients share the struggles of leadership and the challenges to sustain success, I began to see the first two pieces of what would become the larger puzzle. First, a leader can suffer from good ol'-fashioned arrogance. He thinks he knows it all. Once he believes this about himself, it's inevitable that he starts to be condescending to others and impatient with anyone who disagrees with him. At the same time, because he exaggerates his own wisdom, he begins to put less trust in the wisdom of others.

For example, he requires his subordinates to report directly to him, bringing all key decisions back to him for his approval. In doing so, he locks himself into a centralized leadership style.

Such leaders, who pride themselves on their wisdom, really don't know how they come across to others. They think they are helping to get things done but inevitably cause things to slow down. And they also start to lock themselves out of good and useful counsel. The people around them have to focus more on avoiding criticism than excelling in their work, and talent gets dumbed down.

This arrogance also leads to ignorance. When a leader micromanages, he begins to confuse information with insight. He thinks he knows all there is to know about the organization. In his mind, he holds the vault of all there is to know about the organization. But it's impossible for him, or anyone, to have all that. The vault is missing critical documents.

Perhaps this has happened to you as well. When all key decisions come back to you, it requires more meetings, phone calls, e-mails, and correspondence. This means longer days and endless deadlines. As a result, you begin to overwork and fail to nourish yourself because you don't have clearly established work time and personal time. If you've done this, giving all your time to work, you know what every leader has discovered: work expands to fill all the available time given to it. Once you structure your life this way, there is never enough time.

Personal Life Management

Managing personal life is a struggle for every leader I've ever coached in any context. Every leader wants to be large and in charge. To have it all together, to be on top of things, does require a lot of time. And so it's inevitable that the hours will be long—there will always be some tension between the demands of your personal life and your professional life. I always like to remind leaders who talk about their search for balance that the word itself means a resting place between two opposing forces. This is true of leadership. There will never be a time when work and personal life do not compete to some degree for your time and energy. There will always be a tension. The key is to continually replenish your energy to manage the tension well and creatively.

When leaders continue in their same style of work and do not pay attention to the hazards, balance is lost, and their ability to manage their personal life begins to weaken. I see this in the most remarkable ways— not only in what people say, but in their bodies as well. What starts as general overwork or being tired can deteriorate into rashes, sleeping disorders, and even heart issues. Leaders who work ridiculous hours leave little or no time invested in their own health and key relationships. This neglect becomes a nightmare both for physical health and family ties.

The Enemies of Excellence

Most leaders encounter these two basic patterns. Fortunately, we are able to address the egotism and personal life management problems with highly effective solutions that we'll discuss later.

As you look over these first two patterns, you can probably think of many leaders you've known who struggled with them—quite likely, you've struggled with them yourself. And when you or someone else faces these struggles, you don't do so quietly—these kinds of struggles are highly visible and tend to be obvious to many people in the organization. They were also the most obvious to me as I began working closely with leaders as a coach.

As I worked more and more with leaders who were failing in their leadership capacities or destroying their own lives, however, I began to discern more subtle patterns. These were less obvious than others, but every bit as dangerous. Over time, I identified what I will call the Enemies of Excellence. Each of the Seven Enemies builds upon the other. In some cases one at a time, and in other cases all at once, they distract people from being connected in a community of colleagues and move them to an isolated existence where they are destined to make poor decisions, hurt the people around them, and, ultimately,

enemies of excellence

risk levels:

HIGH
Leadership failure
is imminent

MEDIUM
Leadership failure
is elevated

LOW
Leadership failure low
if issues addressed

7 - - - - - - ■ self sabotage

6 - - - - - - ■ isolation

5 - - - ■ broken relationships

4 - - ■ indulgence

3 - - - - - ■ bad habits

2 - - - - - ■ life mismanagement

1 - - - - - ■ egotism

RISK LEVEL EXPLAINED
Leadership risk is driven by ambition to succeed
and failure to address Enemies undermining success.
Leadership risk increases as more Enemies are
active and decreases as Enemies are eliminated.

bring disaster upon themselves. The Enemies of Excellence are real, and they are very dangerous. They are however completely preventable. Let's look at them closely.

The Enemies of Excellence

The following are The Seven Enemies of Excellence, as well as what people who are struggling with the Enemies often say.

- **Enemy One: Egotism.**
   "I know best."
- **Enemy Two: Life Mismanagement.**
   "I'll get to it later."
   "Who has the time?"
- **Enemy Three: Bad Habits.**
   "What harm could it do?"
   "It's just the way I am."
- **Enemy Four: Indulgence.**
   "I just can't help myself."
   "I work so hard, I deserve this reward."
- **Enemy Five: Broken Relationships.**
   "Why don't they just understand me?"
   "I don't really need people."
- **Enemy Six: Isolation.**
   "I can do it on my own."
   "I don't owe you an explanation."
- **Enemy Seven: Self-sabotage.**
   "It's not my fault."
   "I don't know what happened."

Rather than giving you an abstract definition for each Enemy, let me show you how they play out in the life of one leader. Let's revisit Rob's story.

After witnessing the blowup between him and his wife, his colleagues and I began looking back on his leadership. Though we hadn't noticed them at the time, there were many warning signs. One stands out in particular as a clear guidepost for how Rob's life would later unfold. He had low compliance. At one staff meeting, for example, he was the point person for a presentation about how team building required shared commitments to a single set of rules. He discussed the policies regarding standards of conduct—ideas such as avoiding even the appearance of impropriety between management and staff, or men and women. He made a powerful impression, and in the moment he was saying all those words, he probably believed them. But for all his talk about the importance of accountability and high integrity, he never took these words to heart. He allowed himself to bend the rules, which he thought were really intended just for others to follow.

If he'd been a failure at his job from the beginning, he probably would have had to face this problem earlier. His problem might have been clearer to himself and to those around him. But his success became an all-access pass. This is one major reason that high-profile leaders face hazards that can be different, and more extreme, than those facing other leaders. A high-profile leader is surrounded by people who are hungry for the leader's success. They want him to succeed, and if the price for that is to overlook a few red flags here and there, so be it. The greater the success, the greater the danger. Because of Rob's success, for example, he justified his compromising behavior as a reward for all his efforts: "The rules don't apply to me." Rob also demanded higher standards of others that he did for himself. "Do as I say, not as I do." Besides being hypocritical, this inevitably led to resentment from others. In any organization, people quickly notice when the standards are unequal. The resentment that follows leads to isolation.

As well as exhibiting low compliance, Rob also lacked a solid moral foundation—in his case, a healthy fear of God. He justified his behavior by thinking that he was 95 percent good and so it was okay to have a little "naughty" on the side. Respect for people was also a factor. Rob displayed a consistent disconnect between his actions and how they affected other people. His social awareness was weak, and he tended to walk over people, leaving them feeling disrespected. The cumulative effect of these hazards in Rob's leadership led to his decline and ultimate departure from the job.

Tragic Heroes

The decline of a respected leader is so common, so engrained in the fabric of human history, that there is even a term for him—the tragic hero. This type was recognized already in the time of Aristotle. The tragic hero is ". . . a man who is not eminently good and just, yet whose misfortune is brought about not by vice or depravity but by some error or frailty."[1] In other words, he isn't the bad guy in the black hat, and he isn't the good guy in the white hat. He's someone who is at the center of the action—the person we are all rooting for—but, because of weakness, he is going to fall, and fall hard. His abilities are genuine. His fans recognize these abilities and promote him higher and higher. They grant him their allegiance and trust. Later, in an epic moment of weakness, they discover his imperfections, leading to the worst possible conclusions. A lust for power mixed with fatal unresolved flaws builds up like a faulty dam until a structural failure triggers a fall from grace. His devastating mistake is also known as *hamartia*—a Greek term meaning "to miss the mark."

These Enemies of Excellence can affect anyone—from the corner office to the conference room, and from the classroom to the living room.

Rob was a tragic hero. The Board of Directors and staff wanted Rob to win. They had hoped he would be different. His charisma and inspirational leadership were rare. He was so well received by people of all ages because he displayed concern and worked hard to listen. These qualities seemed incompatible with the catastrophe that awaited.

Rob could have won if he'd recognized the hazards inherent in success. Rob overlooked what so many leaders overlook: *you can be in the middle of success and be susceptible to the Enemies of Excellence all at the same time.* There is a path to failed leadership that everyone must understand and proactively avoid.

The path to Rob's failure began, as it does for everyone, when he allowed arrogance into his life. You think your ideas are better than anyone else. You close yourself off from good advice, and so you make rash decisions without the input of others or without listening to the input you've received. You overwork and under-nourish because you require staff to funnel all decisions in the organization back to you. This underutilizes the leaders around you and you lose your best talent or people pull away. You lock yourself into isolation. Your schedule is overfilled because you must manage everything, leaving no time to take care of yourself and your relationships. Your health suffers and you are driven deeper into isolation because of the strains in your key relationships. In this stressed state, destructive habits and behavior patterns from the past emerge, causing even greater guilt, disappointment, and further isolation. Looking for relief, you tamper with temptation. You are now close to destruction. At the crash scene of your life, people wonder how this happened and why a sharp, gifted leader could have acted this way. The pattern, as old as Western civilization itself, repeats itself again and again.

Tragic Headlines

In the wake of failed leadership, we tend to become cynical. We wait for the bottom to fall out, expecting even the best of leaders to fail. The headlines do not offer us hope here, as tragic heroes emerge daily. We live in a day when we discover that even Hall of Fame candidates are really imposters. It becomes increasingly difficult not to look at every prominent figure with great scrutiny. Even a friend or associate can seem marred by their mistakes, and no longer be someone whose success and integrity you will model. Too often, we find that these fatal lapses in judgment war against our struggle for hope. This decline is the death of potential, the shattering of our faith in the great things we wish for in others and ourselves. It is a deep disappointment. Consider the example of one of the most high-profile athletes of our day, Tiger Woods, as we'll look at later. For many people, even those who do not follow golf, he appeared to exemplify virtue and excellence not only on the greens but also in life. With a sigh, we discover that he, too, is a tragic hero. An amazing athlete turned adulterer—another sad example of sexual indecency that violated his wife and children, as well as the millions of people who idolized him.

To make matters worse, as prominent figures make their scandalous falls from glory, they often attribute their misfortune to an "error"—of judgment or circumstances—that is beyond their control. It's rare that they take ownership of the primary cause of their demise. Much of this is the result of self-delusion, but there is an important insight here. Most of them did not consciously set out to fail, and they were genuinely shocked to discover how far gone they were. Their fate was not an error in the sense of a miscalculation, but more the result of neglect: neglect of the flaws in their own hearts and souls and the inherent hazards in leadership and success.

There's a bit of a tragic hero in all of us.

We all have flaws that blind us. If left unattended and unexamined, they will eventually destroy us. One of my own tragic flaws was anger, which affected everything in my life. It nearly destroyed my marriage and estranged my children because I couldn't see it. If I hadn't been confronted with this issue, I would have continued to dismantle and destroy my life and the lives of precious people I love. Fortunately, I recognized my error and learned to alter this destructive behavioral pattern before I alienated everyone and isolated myself.

Up Next

Blindness is widespread today as disgraced leaders sit in the wreckage of their own actions, stunned at their own capacity for deviance. Meanwhile the world looks on with resignation at such leaders. Let's be leaders who determine to be different. Let's join together in becoming leaders who exemplify excellence in who we are and all we do. Let's help each other avoid the hazards of leadership and drive towards sustainable success. Everyone is susceptible to self-sabotage—*especially in the presence of success*. This is why we need each other. There is safety in numbers and in understanding the challenges that face us in our leadership. We can conquer the hazards of leadership and emerge as authentic heroes of our day. But we can't do it through ignorance. To achieve this most noble pursuit will require a greater understanding of the Seven Enemies of Excellence and a resolve to be released from them. If we choose to work on who we are and how we work, we can win. And we must win—our world needs us to do so.

Chapter Three

The Enemy of Egotism

This chapter will equip you to:

- Stop enraging your employees or colleagues and build a culture of collaboration.
- Increase your influence and ability to mobilize team members.
- Enjoy your work and create an environment where people enjoy working with you.
- Become a builder of a great organization, with focus not on yourself but on the greatness of the organization.

Lincoln Hall entered the world with the same guarantee every human being gets—that one day, he would die. In the mind of those who dare to climb Mt. Everest's sheer faces, this possibility looms large, presenting itself in every cautious step, the torrent of an avalanche, and the hostility of subzero temperatures.

With his fellow climbers, the expert Australian climber had just attained the Holy Grail of mountaineering as he stood atop the world's highest peak. This was not the first time he'd tried to achieve the summit, and so this moment was the fulfillment of a long-awaited dream.[1] But he barely lived to savor this victory—during his team's descent, still 28,000 feet above sea level, he was stricken with cerebral edema.[2] What happened next is not shocking to those familiar with Everest ethics. As Lincoln slipped from consciousness, he was left behind for the elements to finish off. Like the empty oxygen tanks discarded by climbers eager to keep their packs light, Lincoln was abandoned by his fellow climbers.

But in the next 24 hours, a miracle occurred. Emerging from unconsciousness for reasons no one can explain, Lincoln battled hallucinations that drove him to the edge of a precipice just two feet wide, with an 8,000-foot drop-off to one side and 6,000-foot fall on the other.[3] There, gripped by severe delusion, Lincoln removed his gloves, hat, and jacket and sat with his hands stretched above his head.

At the same time, American Everest Guide Dan Mazur and his two clients were approaching the location two hours from the summit, and they were shocked to realize that the yellow flash of fabric they spotted atop the ridge was a man.[4] Without any time to prepare for it, they faced an ethical dilemma: complete their journey, which they had invested so much time and money in achieving, or try to save the life of the stranger. Mazur later explained: "You can always go back to the summit, but you only have one life to live. If we had left the man to die, that would have always been on my mind. . . . How could you live with yourself?"[5]

When Mazur reached Lincoln, he realized that this was the same man declared dead by Sherpas more than 12 hours ago. The climbers ministered to Lincoln with their personal supplies of oxygen, food, and water. Through their efforts, Lincoln survived.

Lincoln's rescue stood in stark contrast to the fate of another climber that same year (1984). As solo British climber David Sharp lay dying, he was passed by some 40 climbers on their way to the summit.[6]

In an interview with a New Zealand newspaper, Sir Edmund Hillary, the first man to reach the summit of Mt. Everest (1953), was outraged when hearing of the climbers' passivity toward Sharp. He observed, "people have completely lost sight of what is important . . . In our expedition, there was never any likelihood whatsoever if one member of the party was incapacitated that we would just leave him to die."[7]

This is the exchange of achievement for humanity. The average cost per person of a guided Everest climb is $65,000[8]—but what is the price for a human life? Dan Mazur stood on the winning side of this exchange, even though he risked relinquishing the investments of his clients. But he knows it was worth it. He knows because Barbara Hall still has a husband—and her kids, a father.

Things That Matter

With the lives of altruistic champions as our exemplars, hope has arrived. To deal the fatal blow to egotism, you must identify what you desire as the outcome of your life and leadership. You need to ask yourself: Are you striving to reach just another self-centered summit, or are you leading people and the organization you serve towards something higher? Will you choose an egocentric existence or altruistic excellence?

When we focus on our egos, we tend to think in all-or-nothing terms—"either I achieve this one goal, or I lose everything." But excellence does not work this way. When we decide to do what's right, regardless of the outcome, we will always discover greater opportunity. Let's consider another mountain-climbing story that changed the lives of thousands of children.

In the bestselling book *Three Cups of Tea*, mountaineer Greg Mortenson describes his attempt to climb K2, the second-highest mountain in the world. He became separated from his expedition and was without provisions. Mortenson stumbled his way into the Pakistani village of Korphe. He had promised his dying sister that he would climb K2, but he would never make it back there—he had failed. Yet, as he was being cared for by the Balti people he become fascinated by the children's hunger for knowledge. Their hard work stood in sharp contrast to the extreme lack of resources in their schools, where they learned multiplication tables by scratching the dirt with sticks.

Having failed in one promise, he made another—he promised to build them a school. Despite countless further obstacles, including being kidnapped by the Taliban, Mortenson went on to touch the lives of tens of thousands of children, founding or supporting the work of over 100 schools in those underdeveloped and violent regions. Not bad for "failure."

When we reach for immediate rewards, like the climbers who decided not to help Lincoln Hall, the whole point is missed. Those climbers who reached the summit had achieved their immediate reward alongside more than 2,000 other climbers who have done the same. Whatever praise they receive, in the end, they will be just more names. When it came to what was important, though, both Mazur and Mortenson acted with grace and strength.

Whether it means saving a man's life on a mountain, or putting the needs of others above your own, this heroic and altruistic style of leadership has the highest probability for a positive outcome. Altruists look at fleeting accomplishments and say, "That's great, but I've got something better in mind."

The "something" of greater value is a higher achievement than self-advancement. This is the great foresight of altruists. They clearly see the right choice and invest their time, talents, and treasures accordingly. They don't just live for the now, but for the future and the betterment of themselves and mankind. They understand the welfare and wealth of lifting up a fellow human being.

Jim Collins in his timeless work *Good to Great* discusses the advantages that altruists possess over egotists. His research concludes that when they lead great companies, altruists, or what he calls Level 5 Leaders, "channel their ego needs away from themselves and into the larger goal of building a great company. It's not that Level 5 leaders have no ego or self-interest. Indeed, they are incredibly ambitious—but their ambition is first and foremost for the institution, not themselves."[9]

I have found in my own coaching that when a leader's ambition is focused correctly, he possesses the power of influence—and influence, more than intelligence, is the sign of the greatest leaders.

The attitude of an altruistic leader is infectious—this is what spreads their influence. It infects people with the motivation to achieve the mission of any organization, no matter how hard that may be.

Think of things you've heard people say about the workplace. In an environment led by an egotist, you'll hear:

- "You're here today but may be gone tomorrow."
- "This is a toxic environment."
- "I wish I could leave."

With altruistic leaders, though, you'll hear:

- "They care about us here."
- "This is the best place I've ever worked."
- "I enjoy coming to work, and my work matters."

Let me give you some examples of how egotistical leaders drive an organization.

The Outrage of Egotism

Egotists don't engage in much dialogue. They aren't good listeners and don't truly value your opinion—often, they don't even want it. They have an agenda and want to get it done, now! They literally lock out the distractions of others, even if that includes their colleagues' valuable advice. They are monologue monsters, spilling forth long lists of demands and expecting heads to nod in supportive approval.

Egotists are known to burst into staff members' offices unannounced, with time-sensitive requests, not even sitting down to discuss but rather barking out orders as they march off to the next office to repeat the same behavior. Some egocentric leaders are known to give orders while walking out the door to their next "critically important meeting." Staff disrespect soon turns into resentment and usually removal, as disgruntled employees cease to contribute in their work.

Egotists make people feel expendable. When I coach for organizations, staff will share with me that egotistical leaders have said that staff turnover is "just how we do things." In an ego-driven culture, staff turnover is seen as "what it takes to get the job done." Rob's culture was no different, filled with discontented, discouraged, and disillusioned people. Staff seemed to be buying time until they could find a better alternative and push the Eject button from the insanity they lived every day at work.

The higher you are in an organization, the more harm can reach people. The higher the leader, the more harmful the fall-out will be. There are two reasons.

- First, higher-level leaders make higher-level decisions that affect a broader number of people.
- Second, they are more visible and their mistakes attract greater attention inside and outside an organization. The more public someone is, the less possible it is to deal privately with issues.

Ego-driven leaders not only harm themselves and others—they destabilize and potentially destroy organizations. And once they fall, the fall-out is quite toxic. Here is a recent story that illustrates the devastating effects of an egocentric leader with an egocentric focus. He was an admired entrepreneur, a man who moved elegantly among the esteemed of Wall Street. A picture of the American work ethic, he was chronicled in the *New York Times* for his 70 years of uncommon success. Now he sits disgraced in a prison cell, serving a term much longer than his life, having ruined the financial futures of countless individuals. This is the legacy of Bernard L. Madoff.

Madoff's case vividly illustrates the Enemies of Excellence. He was a micromanager, spending outlandish amounts of money on office renovations and the coordination of his watches and wedding ring.

He could be highly charismatic and kind to the people in his organization, but never shared decision making or control. These are the classic behavior traits I have seen in egocentric high-profile leaders of large organizations. They are charismatic in a public setting and possess a high level of confidence and relentless conviction while manifesting a need to manipulate. They are verbally articulate; their tone of generosity attracts followers, allowing for the advancement of their agenda. This high-level persona requires a high level of control. The leader's purpose appears altruistic, but behind the façade is arrogance with a strong sense of entitlement. Instead of leading a company or cause for the betterment of mankind, a self-centered focus lurks beneath the polished surface.

Madoff, like most egocentric leaders, is highly intelligent. Such leaders befriend people with strong potential within their organization or outside it to secure their plan. "Like a burglar who knows the patrol routes of the police and can listen in on their radio scanners, he also actively wooed regulators who monitored his business."[10] Very diabolical and smart!

All of us know leaders who could have qualified as protégés of Mr. Madoff—masters of manipulation who can think several moves ahead. They plan each self-absorbed action with great precision and excellent execution. They move methodically in manipulation, attempting to shape colleagues into trusted allies who will assist them in their schemes.

Rob is the perfect example of the self-absorbed leader. His time always seemed to be more important that everyone else's. If anyone came in late, he would dismissively say "So glad you could join us," but he himself often came to meetings late. When Rob finally arrived, he wouldn't connect with anyone, and just moved right to business. To make matters worse, he would tend to speak at people rather than speak with them.

For a time, Rob was good at keeping up appearances. He moved with grace and spoke with discernment about how to address major problems the company was facing. Because of his seemingly effortless ability to work under sensitive circumstances, people trusted him more, and he was given greater authority. But problems arose, as they always do with the egotistical leader. In reaction to his dismissive style, dissatisfaction set in, grumbling increased, and factions soon formed. What resulted was a climate of accusation, divided loyalties, and wounded friendships. In meetings, the style seemed easy and in control, but everywhere else, chaos increased. Eventually, the gap between the reassuring surface and the negative results was too great for even his greatest supporters to ignore.

Beware of the discrepancy between what egocentric leaders say and what they do. Beware of this discrepancy in your own leadership as well. If words and actions do not match up, chances are there is a problem. Smooth talk is easy to fall for, especially when a leader consciously appeals to his listener's emotions. To determine a leader's true identity, notice not what he says but how he acts. A leader's identity determines his level of success and the success of the teams or organizations he leads.

The Advantages of Altruism

To avoid the enemy of an egocentric focus, we need to not only determine to avoid egotism but to understand the benefits of altruism. Altruism has great advantages over egotism. Below are several of the benefits I've observed in my work with leaders over the years. Altruistic leaders build sustainable success rather than sabotaging it. Free of the trappings of egotism and arrogance, they can place their best

ALTRUISM	EGOTISM
1. Increased Influence	1. Loss of influence and increased disrespect
2. Holds onto best talent	2. Departure of best talent and difficulty in replacing them.
3. Fosters collaboration	3. Loss of collaboration and rise of discontent
4. Maximizes results	4. Decline in results and decrease in the size and impact of the organization

energy in being an exemplary leader who equips others to achieve exceptional results.

Building an Altruistic Focus

If altruism is to tool for eliminating the egocentric focus in our own lives, how do we build altruism? If you're serious about change, I recommend a process that has proven to be very helpful in moving people from where they are to where they want to be. It's not easy to change our focus, but it can be done. If we engage our will and involve others with a proven process, we can avoid the Enemy of egotism and become an altruistic champion who exemplifies excellence.

The powerful process for change I recommend has the following three steps.

Step One: Evaluate

The purpose of evaluation is to understand your current reality so you can discover the best course for moving forward.

- Complete the Ego Evaluation. To the best of your ability, go with your first impression and try not to over-think each question.
- Now select a few trusted colleagues to evaluate your Ego Evaluation. There is a digital version of the Ego Evaluation as well as many other resources in this book on the *www.coachgreg.com* website under "Tools." Try to select people who are not afraid to be honest with you. Once your colleagues have completed your evaluation, invite them sit down with you one on one and review their evaluation together. Ask them to share examples and suggestions to lower your egotism and increase your altruism. Write notes and ideas on each of the Ego Evaluations to use later in establishing new behavior goals. The goal here is to *raise*

EGO EVALUATION	SCORE
Instructions: In this evaluation, 1 is not correct at all (strongly disagree) and 5 is most correct (strongly agree).	
1. When people are talking, you formulate a response before they are finished.	1　2　3　4　5
2. You find yourself thinking about yourself a lot during the day.	1　2　3　4　5
3. Your needs are more important than those of others.	1　2　3　4　5
4. Your work and achievement comes first and gets the best of your time and energy.	1　2　3　4　5
5. You are a project-before-people person.	1　2　3　4　5
6. You are demanding with people.	1　2　3　4　5
7. It is important that your opinion be considered highly valuable.	1　2　3　4　5
8. You consider your opinion right most of the time.	1　2　3　4　5
9. You will not be overlooked or uninvolved.	1　2　3　4　5
10. You expect a lot from people.	1　2　3　4　5
11. You consider your thoughts and abilities to be superior to most people.	1　2　3　4　5
12. You offer advice even when people are not asking for it.	1　2　3　4　5
13. You consider yourself an expert in most fields.	1　2　3　4　5
14. You drive fast and are late for meetings and personal events.	1　2　3　4　5
15. You struggle to connect in key relationships.	1　2　3　4　5
SCORING	**SCORING INTERPRETATION**
Please add up the total for all 15 questions. You total score is _____.	1. Score of 30 or less is **low** egotism.
	2. Score of 30 to 45 is **medium** egotism.
	3. Score of 45 to 75 is **high** egotism.

your awareness of how you think and behave and how that behavior affects others. View this time as an adventure in learning. It may make you feel somewhat like you are standing naked on a public street, but the incredible gift is personal growth, which will prove very valuable.

Positive Outcomes of Eliminating the Enemy of Egotism

I realize that for many of you, this approach makes you feel highly vulnerable. You are! But it's highly effective in avoiding the dangerous Enemy of Egotism. The vulnerability you model and practice now will increase your value as a person and leader. Vulnerability is an admirable quality that advances your growth and influence as a leader. It also sets you up for greater success in overcoming the other Enemies of Excellence that hinder you in reaching your full potential.

Up Next

At the beginning of this chapter, I identified several benefits you could gain by learning to identify the Enemy of Egotism in your own life. Take a moment now to review those points, before turning to chapter four. There you will encounter The Enemy of Life Mismanagement, which builds on the damage done by the Enemy of Egotism. He is an ominous opponent who outwits millions of people everyday. Be on guard for how you can strengthen your life and avoid the trappings of poor life management that sabotage your success.

Chapter 4

The Enemy of Life Mismanagement

This chapter will equip you to:

1. Build a better balance between your work and personal life.
2. Establish clearer work boundaries.
3. Increase your emotional energy and physical health.
4. Become more productive.

Did you go to the gym this week? Did you eat the food you intended to, or did you end up eating junk? Did you tell your spouse and others in your life how much they mean to you? Did you make time for your kid's game or postpone going for another week?

Like an Egocentric Focus, Life Mismanagement affects most people, even those who seem to have their act together. What makes it so hard to defeat is that it tricks us into thinking it's a time problem, when it's really a priority problem.

The Power of Priorities

Let me explain. Sooner or later, everyone has thought "If only there were more hours in the day, I could . . ." If you think this, then this second Enemy has already gotten to you. Imagine that I have the ability to give you a 30-hour day while everyone else is stuck with the usual 24. Imagine what you could do with the extra time! You could use your extra hours to exercise, prepare fresh food, enjoy a hobby, build richer relationships, and catch up on your sleep. This could revolutionize your life and leadership. You would have greater energy, clarity, and creativity, not to mention a more fulfilled life. You would excel in your professional role and be offered better positions in your field of work. Surely, the extra time would help you become a life management master, wouldn't it?

Actually, it wouldn't. If you aren't establishing your important priorities now with the 24 hours you already have, more time won't help. The people I have coached came to a turning point when they realized that more time was not the answer. The answer lay in establishing important priorities each day—much like identifying sites you want to see on a trip and then driving to them. The people who turned around their life management challenges realized that they were letting everyone and everything in their life drive them. It was time for them to grab the wheel and drive their own lives. When you're in the driver's seat, you can determine what destinations you'll visit that day and what pace you'll take to get there. You set your schedule and allocate your time and resources to the highest priorities in each day. This is how you can secure effective life management and overtake the Enemy.

I want to issue you a life management license today to drive towards better health and productivity. Grab the wheel of your life and set your course each day. Drive to your primary priorities first, and you'll pick up those little things that need to be done while you're driving.

The Enemy of Life Mismanagement can't stand against a person who establishes their priorities and drives towards them each day. He is soon defeated when we make the decision to invest our best energy on top priorities that produce the best personal and professional results.

An Obsession with Control

Rob was not feeling so good.

When we first knew him, Rob had been an inspiration to all of us. He seemed so motivated in all areas of his life, from business to personal. He had a knack for taking care of himself and the people around him. This care was seen in his behavior and even his body. He always dressed well, he ate healthy food, and even though he had a larger frame, he exercised enough that he could tuck his shirt in without showing a belly. He never seemed obsessive, just aware. Every detail was in place.

As time went on, all this changed. He let his physical health deteriorate because he "just didn't have the time." Insufficient sleep intensified the problem as his mind was plagued with too many details that he couldn't turn off. He also couldn't bring himself to turn off his Smart Phone, leading to a constant barrage of phone calls, e-mails, and text messages that breached a necessary boundary between work and rest.

His diet, too, was a disaster. He ate grab-and-go food with too little nutrition to fuel his ferocious drive to succeed. Soon he joined the ranks of the countless zombies who prop themselves up with caffeine and sugar to meet the demands of their lifestyle. Recreation and time with friends became out of the question. Like many others, he thought, "Who's got time to disconnect from work when I'm so important?" His weight began to skyrocket.

It was apparent that Rob had invested little time in effective life management. His entire focus centered on work instead of who he was or, just as importantly, who he was becoming. He worked outrageously long weeks—70 to 80 hours. Because he considered his gifts and abilities to be better than most, he felt he had to place his personal stamp of approval on all decisions. In essence, he was a micromanager, releasing little authority and creating an overwhelming workload of meetings, phone calls, and e-mail correspondence. His obsession with control spun him into chaos. He attributed his lack of delegation to "keeping an eye on everything" and perpetuated what we might call an Atlas mentality. (Atlas was the character in Greek mythology charged with carrying the weight of the heavens for eternity.)

Rob was a *centralized leader*. Because they have not dealt with the egocentric focus, centralized leaders ensure that every key decision comes back to them for their input and final approval. They don't understand that they are the *cause* of their own professional life overload. They cause an overload in meeting attendance, e-mail correspondence, and interruptions because team members and staff must always check their work with the centralized leader before they move forward. This makes a leader feel important, but it is extremely frustrating to staff, and incredibly inefficient.

Every centralized leader battles the Seven Enemies in a different way. Not everyone will become overweight, for example, but a breakdown in life management will leave everyone open to an attack of some kind. As a leader, you too are vulnerable. This Enemy will attack not only your health but your key relationships, emotional stability, and sleeping patterns, increasing your fear, stress, and anxiety levels.

Decentralized leaders, on the other hand, understand the wisdom of empowering team members to lead and make their own decisions. If you have the right people and they are sold on the mission and vision of the organization and understand their roles and responsibilities, let them lead! This is the mindset of a decentralized leader. In this approach, as shown on the next page, the leader becomes a coaching leader who builds strong leaders, cohesive teams, and a highly collaborative culture, leading to better life management for himself and others, and exceptional results as well.

Systematic Renewal

I know that becoming a decentralized leader is not easy. Most of us struggle with disconnecting from the professional demands in our life. It is the dilemma of our day. I have been there, and my health, relationships, and professional performance suffered just as Rob's did. How do I get everything done and thrive as a person doing it? I've found a solution that saved me from this Enemy and has helped others build sustainable success as well.

centralized vs. decentralized

LEADERSHIP STYLES

Centralized leaders control and frustrate, while decentralized leaders empower people.

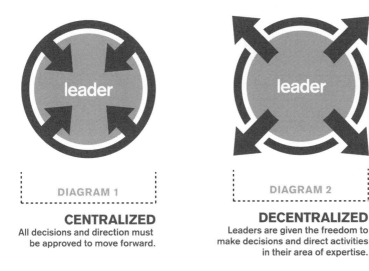

DIAGRAM 1	DIAGRAM 2
CENTRALIZED	**DECENTRALIZED**
All decisions and direction must be approved to move forward.	Leaders are given the freedom to make decisions and direct activities in their area of expertise.

The solution is quite simple, really. *Replace the energy you expire.* I call the solution *systematic renewal*. Systematic renewal is the powerful process by which we engage in replenishing activities to continually recover the energy we're consuming. This continual state of renewal results in living and leading from a position of strength— our Ideal Health State. It is an effective counter-attack to the Enemy of life mismanagement. The Ideal Health State is achieved when our spiritual, emotional/mental, relational, and physical tanks are full. This positions us to overcome the Enemy.

systematic renewal

OPTIMUM HEALTH

Optimum Health is achieved when spiritual, emotional, relational and physical health are replenished.

Systematic renewal begins as you determine the specific activities that provide replenishment in the four areas of Optimum Health. In my case, for example, I need to begin my day with some time for reflection. I like being in a quiet place to read, think, and pray. I then move directly into planning to ensure that my day has a clear focus with clear targets to achieve. I head to the office and stay focused on my daily plan, knowing that I have a personal break at lunch. Lunch is a critical time of day for me. I need a mental and emotional break and time to recharge my energy for an effective afternoon. A lunchtime workout with a quick shower significantly improves my productivity in my afternoons. I mix up the workouts to ensure they are fun. I like to bike, run, swim, or lift weights. I always try to include a friend to maintain motivation. The lunchtime exercise is highly effective in learning to disengage from the professional side of life. It reinforces shifting from work to replenishing activity and back to work again. The shift is absolutely critical in maintaining effective life management.

When I get back to the office after lunch, I'm ready to dive into my work and knock out my remaining priorities before heading home for family dinner. Dinners have always been a great tradition in my life to connect with family and share the day. This comes from my Italian upbringing—for us, dinner was an experience that involved fantastic food and funny stories. We laughed, we cried, we argued, we lived life and loved it. Today these meals remain critical in building connections with the special people in my life. After dinner, we go on walks or play games. Vacations and special occasions have also played an important part in keeping me connected to family and friends. There were many years we could not afford a vacation, so our family worked together cleaning an office to earn the money to go. My wife entered and won contests that sent us on incredible vacations around the world. Birthdays and anniversaries need to be celebrated. This is life and we need to live it! Now! Not later when work allows. Have you noticed that work is always present and, like fire, is never satisfied? You can't let it define your life for you.

One Story of Renewal

Last year Dianna and I celebrated our 25th wedding anniversary. We went to our favorite island, Kauai. Little did we know as we lifted off from SeaTac Airport that there was a surprise waiting for both of us. In the first few days of our trip, we dug our toes into the soft sand and enjoyed snorkeling and hiking around the island. Then the night came for us to celebrate our 25 years together as a married couple. We got dressed up and headed to a special restaurant. Dianna had a surprise waiting for me. "Guess what? We're going down to the beach, and a pastor is going to help us renew our vows."

We made our way to the front of a beautiful old church where a Hawaiian pastor greeted us. We stood on a cliff overlooking Shipwreck Beach. The sun was setting and the warm breeze off the ocean refreshed us as we looked into each other's eyes. The Hawaiian pastor blew a large seashell sending beautiful deep tones into the air to announce our marriage celebration. Each part of the ceremony was a special moment that built our love and brought us closer.

In the middle of the ceremony, the pastor asked if we would be exchanging rings. Dianna had lost her diamond a few years earlier, and at the time we were busy putting kids through an expensive college—a replacement ring with a real diamond just wasn't in the budget. Without Dianna knowing it, though, I had been saving for some time and bought her a new ring with three diamonds. There was a stone for each of our two sons, and the one in the middle represented our love for each other. I wasn't sure when I'd have the chance to show it to her. So I wish you could have seen her face, and mine, when the pastor gave me the perfect opening and said, "Will you be exchanging wedding rings now?" Dianna said that we'd already exchanged rings when we were married. Thinking on my feet, I said: "Well actually, I do have a new ring for Dianna." I pulled out the black velvet box and opened it to reveal the ring and place it on her finger. It was a great moment and an amazing evening we both will remember forever.

You need to celebrate such occasions in your own life as well. Special moments bond us together like nothing else. We need them in our lives. They provide a unique opportunity for us to connect at the heart, and the more connected we are to significant people in our life, the safer we are from Enemy attack.

In my experience, closely connected relationships are our most important priority. They are the best strategic tactic a leader can use to destroy all the Enemies of Excellence. In my work with fallen leaders, there is always a common risk factor: *isolation*. As we'll see later, their egotistical focus, combined with a breakdown in life management and the other five Enemies, drives them deep into solitary confinement where they act out in audacious and outrageous behavior. And every one of them wonders how they got there! It's really no mystery. They replaced work for connected, caring relationships.

The Turning Point

You can turn it around. I have. I haven't always had the healthy life management pattern I've described here. There were many dark days as an egotist that I would rather not remember. My lack of effective life management almost dissolved my marriage and destroyed my family.

Will there be consequences to your mistakes? Yes! There always are, and their severity depends on how many Enemies you allow to operate in your life. But it is possible to turn things around, and the earlier you recognize The Enemies of Excellence, the better. That's how my turnaround started: *recognition*.

I was fortunate. I had exceptional friends, coaches, and mentors who helped me recognize the Enemies that were active in my life and were taking me and my family down. I began to see how my egotistical focus closed my mind to hearing sound advice. I was missing insight from very smart people all around me. I also learned that I was constantly filtering conversations and only picking up on bits and pieces, usually missing the meaning of what people were really saying. In seeing what I was missing I was beginning to escape from the powerful Enemy of Egotism.

My life management skills began to change when I was recovering from back surgery. I determined during physical therapy that I would learn how to be healthy. I promised myself at that moment not only to be physically healthy, but to have a healthy heart and head. I launched on a learning journey with the aim of doing life differently. That was 17 years ago, and I'm still learning and growing. It takes a lot of practice to build effective life management.

That's the second secret of turnaround: *practice*. Every year I learn new ways of being the best person I can possibly be. It's important to always be learning and growing, and to be willing to abandon those things that no longer work or are outdated.

This leads us to the third turnaround tactic: *be innovative*. When you start doing something a lot, you'll always find better ways to do it. Be innovative in trying new approaches to exercise, or connecting with the key people in your life. Just remember, it's in the doing that you discover new approaches.

Life Management Best Practices

There are life management patterns that I see practiced in leaders who have learned how to build sustainable success. Here are a few best practices to consider.

These leaders tenaciously:

- Establish work boundaries.
- Schedule vacations and personal planning times a year in advance.
- Invest mornings in uninterrupted, high-priority activity.
- Engage in daily exercise, providing emotional and mental relief as well as energy replenishment.
- Use the afternoons for management, including meetings, phone calls, and e-mail.
- Guard evenings and weekends for relationship connection and personal enjoyment.
- Invest in outside insight from mentors, coaches, and trainers focusing on personal and professional growth.

Mastering Life Management

I recommend three steps in moving towards life management mastery. First, determine your priorities, then build a plan to achieve them, and finally practice achieving them each day. Let's take one at a time and prepare you today to launch into greater life management success.

Step One: Determine Priorities

You've heard me discuss earlier how I started my own turnaround in life management. I needed to recognize the priority gaps in my life. When we can clearly see and understand a problem, we are much closer to solving it. You'll need the outside insight of others to achieve this first step. Ask yourself and others close to you: "What does my behavior say about

PERSONAL PRIORITIES	PROFESSIONAL PRIORITIES
Recommendations • Practice daily Reflection time. • Practice daily Planning time. • Practice daily Exercise time. • Schedule all personal time in master calendar, including days off, vacations, time with friends, and personal planning times. • Purchase and prepare fresh food daily. Target 5-7 servings a day of fruits and vegetables. Bring food to work. Ensure you are properly hydrated with 6–8 glasses of water a day. • Engage in ongoing personal growth through a mentor, trainer, or professional coach. • Guard evenings and weekends for relationship connection and personal enjoyment. Ensure you are not isolated from connected caring relationships that provide accountability.	Recommendations • Established work hours. • Practice daily uninterrupted project time (3-4 hours). Schedule project time as an appointment in your calendar. • Engage in ongoing professional growth through a mentor, trainer, or professional coach. • Plan your week each week before it begins, considering personal and professional responsibilities. Enter all priorities in master calendar as appointments. • Ensure the roles and responsibilities of your job are clear. Stay in your area of expertise, and whenever possible, delegate.
Your Personal Priorities 1. 2. 3. 4. 5. 6. 7.	Your Professional Priorities 1. 2. 3. 4. 5. 6. 7.

my priorities in life?" "What established priorities are serving me well?" "What areas of my life need attention?" "How can I practice greater Systematic Renewal and build Optimum Health?" Make a list of your personal and professional priorities below.

Step Two: Plan Priorities

Planning needs to be very simple, or we abandon it. Once your priorities are selected, determine what supplies you need to achieve them. For example, if you're going to exercise each day, you need your gear in a bag in the car. If it's not there, you won't do it. The same is true of great nutrition. If you're going to eat fresh food, it will need to be purchased, prepared at home, and brought with you to work. The planning principle I am describing is called *staging*. To stage is to supply everything you need for each priority. In a triathlon race, you stage your transition area so that when you get out of the water, your bike, shoes, and helmet are ready to go. And when you return from the biking leg, your running shoes are staged for you to transition to the final part of the race. Your race will be successful if you stage well, or a complete failure if you don't. The same is true of our lives. Imagine how your life management success would increase if you staged better. Imagine if you staged your personal and professional priorities by supplying everything you needed for them. You will discover, as many people have, that you have much more potential for success than you

PRIORITY PLAN	STAGING
SUPPLIES	PLACEMENT OF SUPPLIES
1. Example: Gym bag.	1. Car.
2.	2.
3.	3.
4.	4.
5.	5.
6.	6.
7.	7.
8.	8.
9.	9.
10.	10.

are utilizing today. At first, staging is a bit awkward, but over time it becomes quite natural. Invest a few minutes now in creating your staging list, and prepare for launching your priorities.

Step Three: Practice Priorities

Practice doesn't make things perfect—it makes them permanent. Permanence is what we need in our priorities to build sustainable success. You have selected your personal and professional priorities and have your supplies ready and know where and when to have everything staged. In this step, you encounter your greatest obstacle: you. The practice stage requires the building of discipline, and discipline for all of us is difficult. The best way to build discipline is to have some early wins. Start with the priorities you're most confident in achieving. Practice them first, and let yourself win with them. Then slowly begin to incorporate other priorities as you're able to focus on them. Remember: effective life management and sustainable success is a marathon, not a sprint. It will take years to build mastery in this area, and patience will become a virtue in this process. When you fail, fail forward and begin again the next day. Failure is necessary for further growth. You will be faced over and over with the choice to turn your failure into fuel to move onto the next level of growth—or to let failure foil you. I know you will win!

Additional Growth

If you're interested in further growth, please visit *www.coachgreg.com* for information on what it takes to have a professional coach to assist your personal growth.

Up Next

At this point, you've had the chance to witness the four benefits mentioned at the beginning of this chapter, and soon you'll be able to experience them in your own life, as you do the activities suggested here and begin to get your life back into balance. You'll need the lessons of this chapter as we move into the next chapter and cross over to the dark side of the soul. We will discover what happens in a person's life when they allow the Enemies of Egotism and Life Mismanagement to exist. It's a bit scary, so buckle your seat belts.

Chapter Five

The Enemy of Bad Habits

This chapter will equip you to:

- Understand why bad habits exist.
- Be more intentional with your day to increase your productivity and the achievement of priorities.
- Replace bad habits with good ones.

Everyone has a bad habit. Some are more obvious than others. Have you ever seen a child pick his nose in public? He's just digging and digging, and out pops something that no human wants to see except the youngster who just found it. How about cussing? People who cuss speak a different language. Every other word has an expletive in it, and they aren't able to communicate without using some choice word every few seconds. If you ask them to stop, they don't know what to do. They look at you like you're crazy. "This is how I express myself. It's who I am."

Other habits are less obvious—like lying. There's stretching the truth a bit to add some color to your story. That's to be expected, right? You've gone fishing and you want your friends to enjoy your story and be proud of the monster fish you caught. It was really a baby fish that barely bent the tip of your pole, not a 10-pounder that almost got away after an hour of trying to pull it in. Everyone knows that you're stretching the truth, but you're still stretching the truth, and it's still a bad habit.

I have some bad habits of my own, and one of them is the need for speed.

The Need for Speed

I drive fast. It's a bad habit and hard to break. I grew up in the 70's during the muscle car era with a group of high school buddies who loved to build street rods. We didn't have much cash, but our cars could get up and go.

My need for speed started when my dad moved our family out of Burbank, California to a small town in the high desert above Palm Springs, where everything revolved around football and fast cars. For a small high school, it was surprising how the expectations to excel were high in both academics and athletics. You were expected to hit the books and hustle in practice. I learned a lot. When we were done with our studying, we would take some time to tinker with our cars. Our auto shop teacher was a bit of a speed enthusiast. He didn't just teach us how to change the oil in our cars—he helped us build some machines that were fast in the quarter mile.

Friday nights in the fall were fun! First, we did our best to beat the visiting team, then we grabbed our girlfriends for a night on the town to see who had the hottest car. My blue beauty was a '68 fastback Mustang with a 351 Cleveland under the hood. It was powered with 300 ponies that pounced on some pretty tough competition. I didn't always win, but I sure made a good showing as long as my car held together.

Street racing was fun, but definitely a bad habit. It's dangerous, and many things can go wrong in a very short amount of time. It can also get you into a lot of trouble, as most bad habits can. One day during my senior year I was at the Dairy Queen eating burgers with friends. As I was leaving the parking lot, I just had to spin the tires a bit before I merged into traffic—not the smartest thing to do in the middle of the day. I turned the corner toward the high school when an officer flashed his lights and pulled me over. I thought to myself—no, not another ticket! I'd already had a steady stream of speeding violations that were rapidly burning up my paychecks. Between the gas, tires, repairs, and tickets, this bad habit was beating me up.

That's the way bad habits work. They're a lot of fun—that's why they became habits in the first place. But they always have a high price tag, for us and for the people that are connected to us. In some cases, the cost can be even higher—my need for speed could have cost me my life and the lives of my friends. Bad habits not only consume our resources; they put us at risk and contaminate our lives.

Looking back, of course, I can clearly see how I had gone too far. On top of schoolwork, leadership activities, and playing three sports a year, I was working evenings and weekends mainly to support an expensive car. Crazy! I had very little free time and this created a steady stream of stress. But I had built an image for myself around being an athlete and driving a hot car. Of course, the problems did not stop there. The Enemy of Egotism got an early grip in my life and encouraged me to elevate myself above others. My anger would rage when people failed to meet my expectations, and every time I created a mess, I would find myself saying, "It's not my fault."

Why did I do this to myself? Why do any of us allow bad habits to consume our lives?

Why Bad Habits Exist

I often see the same patterns when working with leaders. They are struggling with the Enemy of Bad Habits, or worse, they have resigned themselves to their bad habits and stopped struggling at all. They have bought into the lie "it's not my fault." In my experience over the last two decades, there are specific reasons why they struggle with the Enemy of Bad Habits.

Bad Habits exist because:

- We're lazy and lack discipline. (For example, we fail to plan our day, and because of our lack of discipline we inevitably fail.)
- We are looking for an escape from the stress and routine

of life. We waste productive time in surfing the Internet, interrupting coworkers, playing video games, or watching TV.

- We are tired and worn out. We don't eat well, hydrate, exercise, or get enough sleep, and so we suffer for it.
- We lack the conviction that a bad habit exists. We are denial specialists and seek to project our struggles on other people—it's somehow "their fault."
- We "don't care." We're either too depressed, rebellious, or lazy. We don't believe we can change or don't believe the situation can change. (We need to build up our "believability" and take steps of change.)
- We are afraid of change because if we "do things differently" we might make a mistake. (Of course, yes, we will continue to make mistakes, but the fact that we are trying is what has always moved people towards excellence. Overcome the fear of failure with focused effort.)
- We aren't trained well in an area of life or leadership. (Overcome this excuse by getting the training you need, now.)
- We're running too fast to evaluate our efforts and see areas of inefficiency and ineffectiveness. (Plan first, then proceed.)
- We're following the wrong leadership advice or people. (Test everything you learn before you adopt it.)
- We're carrying bad behavior patterns from the past into the present. (Face them and fill your future with good behaviors that replace the bad ones.)

All the bad habits we have identified can be overcome. The question to ask yourself is—are you willing?

There is one other in addition to all these reasons. The primary reason that we are overrun by the Enemy of Bad Habits has to do with *intentional versus reactionary living*. Here's an example: the more intentional we are in planning our week, the more productive we will be. When we have clear targets to hit each day, we will be better at navigating around the distractions and interruptions we encounter. Intentionality places us in a position to be productive with our personal and professional priorities. We can stay on course in our day and avoid getting lost. Intentionality moves us to a place of work/life balance. There is an ancient proverb that supports this strategy.

"Wise people think before they act; fools don't and even brag about it!"
(Proverbs 13:16 NLT)

Wise people think through their actions. They are constantly identifying bad habits and moving to eliminate them from their daily actions. When we are not intentional, we fall prey to the tyranny of the urgent—we end up acting in response to whatever seems most pressing in the moment. But in the absence of intentionality, *everything* seems urgent, and we stand there frozen like a deer in the headlights right before he gets run over. We run from task to task, spinning around like we're on a merry-go-round and wondering when we can get off.

As things progress, we might even take pride in how "out of control" and crazy our lives have become. In Rob's case, for example, he would brag about how the ridiculous hours he was working had caused him to develop bad habits. It was as though his schedule had a mind of its own, taking shape with no input from him, and he was its victim and just had to live with his bad habits. I would hear him say, "It's just the way it is." My reply was always: "It is really the way you make it." We train ourselves—and, too often, others—to suppose that reactionary leadership is a reality separate from our own decisions. In fact, it's a reality you can choose. Or not choose. I recommend that you reject it. To react is to reduce excellence and invite other Enemies. Reactionary leadership reduces our ability to make better decisions, gain good counsel, and stay on a clear course.

Overcoming Bad with Good

The first step in choosing intentional leadership lies in a simple but powerful best practice: overcome bad habits with good ones. Don't waste your time focusing on the problem, but rather build the solution that will replace the problem. Once you identify a bad habit, determine what good habit to put in its place. Then focus your energy on building your good habits. What you will find in time is that you abandon a bad habit, not out of increased willpower, but because it is now obsolete. You don't want or need it any longer.

This simple solution does require a key ingredient: *diligence*— remaining focused on the new habit and finding ways throughout the day to reinforce it. Diligence becomes a delight when it's deployed. To be diligent is to be strict and sharp with your actions. You are focused on forging something of great worth. You see a prize in your pursuit. Another ancient proverb casts light on the importance of diligence:

"The plans of the diligent lead to profit as surely as haste leads to poverty."
(Proverbs 21:5 NIV)

We can lead to profit if we are willing to build a plan and be diligent. But be warned that the Enemy of Bad Habits will tempt you with haste so that you waste your efforts. He hates excellence and will do whatever he can to encourage you to shortcut your diligence. He uses thoughts like the following:

- "This is taking too long."
- "There must be an easier, faster way."
- "Why try? I've had this bad habit for a long time, and it's never going to go away."
- "Look, no one's perfect. Don't worry—a few bad habits won't hurt you. Let it go, and don't push yourself so much to change."

Learn to ignore these thoughts by focusing on the positive goal. And don't get discouraged. Remember that you have practiced your bad habits a long time. It will take just as long or longer to replace them with good ones. Build a good plan, get some solid counsel, and go for it!

Moving from Bad to Good

Excellence is earned! I encourage you to invest a few minutes in building your plan to blast the bad habits from your life. In the chart below, list your bad habits in both your personal life and your professional leadership. Then determine what good habits you would like to build to replace the bad. Consider the action steps you will take each day to establish your good habits. In chapter seven you will be encouraged to share this plan and others with a Core Group of trusted advisors to increase your success. Enjoy your efforts as you remove the bad habit barriers that block your success.

Up Next

The first three Enemies—Egotism, Life Mismanagement, and Bad Habits—are common among most leaders. And by completing exercises like the one you just did, you discover how they relate to your own life. Luckily, these three Enemies are easier to address and overcome.

BAD HABITS	GOOD HABITS	DAILY ACTIONS
Personal Life 1. 2. 3. 4.		
Professional Leadership 1. 2. 3. 4.		

The more lethal Enemies—Indulgence, Broken Relationships, Isolation, and Self-Sabotage—are far more challenging and can cause considerable collateral damage. They have proven throughout history to bring down even the most dedicated and talented leaders. Rigor is the key to avoiding their mistakes. My encouragement to you as you progress through chapters six through nine is to be brutally honest with your personal evaluations and exercises. Your sustainable success depends on it.

Chapter Six

The Enemy of Indulgence

This chapter will equip you to:

- Identify the indulgences that undermine your success.
- Develop a plan to eliminate excess in your life.
- Determine the character traits that will deter indulgence and drive you towards excellence.

The headline reads "Woods Seems Lost with No Way Out." Tiger Woods is at the Bridgestone Invitational and is struggling at his game, having just shot his worst score as a pro and trying to avoid last place. Tim Dahlberg a national sports columnist for *The Associated Press*, notes "Suddenly, his whole legacy is in as much jeopardy as his once pristine image. Once thought to be a cinch to break Jack Nicklaus' record [for major tournament victories] and be declared the greatest golfer ever, Woods has lost both his mystique and his confidence."

How did one of golf's greatest champions dismantle his career?

Was it his practice schedule? Once known to be a practice fanatic, had he let his fame interfere with his work ethic? Has he lost his passion to pursue excellence? In any case, he is now paying a high price for repeatedly cheating on his wife. The Enemy of Indulgence has added another notch to his belt. Tiger Woods now goes home to an empty house with no hugs from a beautiful family—a high price tag for a little pleasure.

A High Price to Pay

A great champion is now reaping what he sowed. That's the problem with indulgence, whether it affects a superstar or those less famous. Each indulgent action plants a seed of destruction. Tiger still has the talent and experience to be a champion, but there are too many toxic weeds in his life. He's burdened with the weight of his wrong decisions. No wonder it's so hard for him to focus his game performance.

Anyone who engages in indulgence soon discovers how debilitating it can be. Whether the indulgence is food, alcohol, substance abuse, or sexual indiscretion, it always ends the same—a desperate existence. Take a moment and reflect on family, friends, coworkers, political leaders, sports figures, entertainers, spiritual leaders and historical characters. Has Indulgence ever produced better people? No. This ominous Enemy encourages people to exchange their life for destruction—their personal destruction, but also the destruction of family, friends, colleagues, and organizations related to them.

Don't make the mistake of assuming that this happens only to others. Pause for a moment to reflect on this: What are you sowing and reaping? Are you engaging in some form of indulgence? To answer this more clearly, invest in your excellence and complete the following Indulgence Inventory. Use this exercise to eliminate any Indulgence that is undermining your success.

This is a defining moment. If your life is free of Indulgence at this time, great! If not, you have a decision to make. You can make a decision to face your Indulgence and work towards elimination, or you can allow it to continue to contaminate you. Your decision will determine the direction of the rest of your life. I encourage you to face your Indulgence and invite the help of trusted friends or advisors. I have, and I found it to be very effective in overcoming areas in my life that weighed me down. Let this be a time of turnaround and determine today to contact two people who can assist your passion to purify your life.

Indulgence Inventory

Indulgence means yielding to your desires, resulting in excess that undermines your success. In the following inventory consider three things:

1. *Where* are you indulging? (Examples: excessive food, alcohol, recreation, sex, spending, etc.)
2. *How* are you indulging? What activities are you engaging in that facilitate your indulgence?
3. *What* will you do to eliminate your indulgence? What actions will you take to remove the excess from your life?

Where are you indulging?	*How* are you indulging?	*What* will you do to eliminate indulgence?
1. Food	1.	1.
2. Alcohol	2.	2.
3. Recreation	3.	3.
4. Sex	4.	4.
5. Spending	5.	5.
6. [Other] _____	6.	6.
7. _____	7.	7.

The Contamination of Conscience

Think back to Rob. He was exchanging his life for destructive behavior, but he didn't know how to stop. What concerned him was that he lacked the willpower to want to change. And it's easy to see why. Over time, he came to be surrounded by women eager to spend time with him, be in his presence, and help him in whatever ways they could. Eventually, he reciprocated the attention, to the point that others in the office began to be uncomfortable with the environment.

The sequence after that was a pattern I've observed too many times in these situations. What begins as flirting in the office graduates to calls, emails, and text messages, then private lunches or secret meeting places, where the two people can explore their desires without anyone knowing. That is, they delude themselves that no one knows—the behavior is usually obvious to everyone else.

This pattern fits the promiscuous behavior that Rob displayed. In experimenting with sexual indulgence, he discovered how easy it was to override the red flags in his conscience by giving into his desires. Even though he felt in control, to the point that he viewed these conquests as a game, in fact the game had conquered him. Now he found himself enslaved in his desires.

The Enemy of Indulgence works that way. It helps you dismantle your conscience piece by piece until the alarms of moderation or morality are silenced. With the alarm system disabled, all kinds of destructive behavior can be explored.

We contaminate our conscience every time we decide to partake of forbidden fruit. Whether it's Adam and Eve in the garden or a young executive on a business trip, people know that forbidden fruit is forbidden for a very good reason—it poisons your passion, perspective, and purpose. Forbidden fruit harms you and make you a fool. No one wants to be a fool, but when you think about it, the most dangerous behaviors are all very foolish—it's preposterous to do them. No one sets out in their life and says; "Today I'm going to do my best to sabotage my success. I think I will embrace indulgence and see how much damage it can do to my life and the people around me." And yet, many people go out and do exactly that, every day. Why?

How the Enemies Gain Ground

Look at the first three Enemies of Excellence. As egotism is allowed to exist, it breeds arrogance, and arrogance in turn builds ignorance.

People become ignorant of the other Enemies that are active in their life and leadership. The second Enemy ensures that the balance between work and life is ignored and allowed to break down. As work-life balance breaks down, bad habits accumulate. This third Enemy opens the door to the dark side of Indulgence. And as we have discussed in this chapter, the Enemy of Indulgence creates heavy casualties.

Each time you encounter an enemy, a defining moment emerges. Will you decide to turn around, or drive further into disaster?

Why do we let the Enemies of Excellence gain ground in destroying our lives? There are three reasons.

The first reason is *pride*. People in general are proud, and those who lead are even more so. It's very hard to admit when we're wrong, and this only gets harder and harder the higher you rise in life and leadership success. I have found that many people would rather be wrong than right, if being right requires them to let go of their pride, and this drives them deeper into the Enemies of Excellence. I have worked face to face with very intelligent people who will indignantly defend their destructive behaviors. Whether it's blowing their top in a meeting or giving themselves special privileges no one else is allowed to have, they dismiss any attempt to confront their poor choices while they drive themselves and their organizations off the cliff.

While most of us are familiar with pride, the second reason is not as obvious. It's a lack of *understanding*. We live in a world governed by cause and effect. As Newton taught us, every action creates a reaction. Imagine jumping into a small boat from the shore. As you jump into it, the boat will sway from side to side and everything in it will be in motion. This truth about physics is true in life and leadership as well. I was recently consulting with a leader who walked into a meeting and soon began disrespecting his top team members. I watched their facial expressions slowly change from excitement to disappointment, disengagement, and disgust. The oxygen was sucked out of the room.

The third reason is *experience*. In my own work, I needed outside insight from others. We are all very limited in our own life experience, and I knew I needed to expand mine. Fortunately, some incredible men came into my life who vastly improved my scope of experience. They taught me what they had learned, and I was able to add that to my own experience. They challenged me in ways that no one had ever done before, and this too enhanced my experience. Their coaching led me to become a better husband, father, leader, and professional coach. They helped me learn the secrets of sustainable success.

The Antidote for Indulgence

There is a powerful defense for defeating the Enemy of Indulgence. It's character. Our character contains our moral and ethical qualities. The stronger it is, the greater defense it offers. The weaker it is, the more susceptible to sabotage we become.

The best way to build character is to define it, practice it, and defend it. Once you define your character so that you clearly understand it, you can practice it in everyday life and leadership. This increases your character competency and prepares you to defend it when you face the Enemy of Indulgence.

In the following exercise you'll define the character traits that already exist in your life and consider other character traits you would like to add. As you define your character traits, you are building your personal Character Code. A Character Code is a set of standards that defines who you are and how you act. It forms your reputation and, more importantly, what indulgent behavior you refuse to engage in. Enjoy this exercise, and know that you're building sustainable success and enduring excellence. I have included a sample for your consideration; others can be found at *www.coachgreg.com* under "Tools."

Character Code

Character Trait	Description	Life Expression
1. Moderation	I will practice restraint and avoid excess.	I will practice portion control in my eating and limit my spending with an established budget.
2.		
3.		
4.		
5.		
6.		
7.		

Up Next

Have you ever wondered why key relationships breakdown? Our next Enemy, the Enemy of Broken Relationships, loves to separate friends and sabotage couples. As you move into the next chapter, I encourage you to be courageous and confident as you seek to build connected, caring relationships.

Chapter Seven

The Enemy of Broken Relationships

This chapter will equip you to:

- Determine what is most valuable to you.
- Remove the barriers that break down your key relationships.
- Build your Core Group of trusted advisors to enhance your life through insight, support, care, and accountability.

As Rob continued to unravel, he made many mistakes, but his greatest was to isolate himself. Connection with others is the final safety net keeping leaders out of the hands of Enemies Six and Seven. Rob was disconnecting. He would go for weeks at a time without any down-time and no real conversation with others except related to work. Even as family members and board members approached him, he gave them standard responses: "This is just a busy season . . . I just have a lot to do . . . I don't have time—it will all be over soon." Be aware that this is a difficulty with many leaders. No matter how much you try to intervene and assist them, they will resist your input. They believe they have to do it on their own.

Rob struggled to spend quality time with his wife and kids. He treated family like just another project to manage, another task to check off his list, and it showed. He became emotionally and mentally withdrawn. You could see it in his demeanor. He didn't smile the way he used to. His playful, teasing style was gone. He was tense and easily irritated. He was disconnected and distracted most of the time. The Enemy of Broken Relationships was digging in and working hard to cut every last connection to key relationships. Rob was quickly being surrounded by the Enemies of Excellence. He was being cornered and cut off from anyone who could help him. He was isolated, vulnerable, and very alone, but his brain was too distracted to see it.

A Resurrected Relationship

By this point, Rob was a mess. It's easy for us to read Rob's story and think of him as someone else, but the Enemies he was facing affect all of us. Earlier, I wrote about the magical vacation I spent with my wife, where we renewed our vows to each other after 25 years. It was a sacred moment that we both will never forget. But what I didn't mention is that we almost didn't make it. Years earlier, Dianna came to me one day and said "I'm done!" She meant it. We had grown apart and had not placed the value we should have on our relationship. It's not that we didn't give of ourselves, but we'd poured our best into our work, our boys, and everyone else, not into each other. Our relationship was on the rocks and soon would be washed away forever.

We needed help, so we reached out to our Board of Directors, family, friends, and an excellent counselor. It was a lot of work, but over a period of two years we learned how to build a dynamic marriage from a dying one.

I would never want to have to live through that time again, but something good did come of it—I learned how to be a better man and husband. I learned that there was a large gap between how much I said I valued our relationship and how much I actually invested in it. I learned that as a hard-driving achiever, my tendency is to place projects before people, and this is a mistake—relationships don't wait. At any moment, we are either enriching and building them or losing them.

I learned the hard way, having to face the bitter prospect of a failed marriage. Rob learned an even harder way, as he fell into adultery, isolation, and the destruction of all his key relationships.

How about you? How valuable are relationships to you? You don't have to wait to deal with the fifth Enemy and strengthen this aspect of your excellence. You can address it immediately.

What Do You Value?

What in your life is important, so important that you can't live without it? It's a great question to ask yourself. Please list below the top ten things that are most valuable to you in your life.

My Most Valuable Things

1.
2.
3.
4.
5.
6.
7.
8.
9.
10.

Now look back over that list, and put a check by your top three most valuable things. Finally, circle the most valuable thing in your entire life. Take a few minutes and write down why your number one area is so valuable to you.

_____

_____

_____

_____

_____

_____

What do you think? Do you currently value what you want to value? How high are key relationships on your list? It's important to know, because how you value relationships and engage in building and maintaining them is absolutely critical to your sustainability and success.

How you value relationships also determines how well you defend yourself against the Fifth Enemy. This Enemy is the relationship wrecker. He loves to destroy marriages and see children hurt. He wants to isolate people so that they are easy targets to be taken out. He strives to poison the key connections in your life.

His plan of attack is to have you exchange your key relationships for personal indulgence and professional achievement. He works best with the leaders who want special "rewards" for their hard work, those who are driven to "get it done at any cost"—that cost inevitably being colleagues, friends, marriages, and children.

The "at any cost" leader is easy prey for this Enemy because he carries a lot of false beliefs:

- "The job requires me to work all the time."
- "Yes, I work too much, but it's short-term, just for this season."
- "My key relationships will wait for me to reemerge from my excessive work."
- "The key people in my life must understand the demands of my work and my need to succeed. I can make it up to them later."

Such a leader doesn't recognize that an egocentric focus combined with a breakdown in work life balance, bad habits, and indulgence will lead to ruined relationships that cannot be replaced. As he is climbing to the top of the next hill of achievement, he is leaving more and more people behind, people who care for him, love him, and want to share life with him. He is moving to that deadly place of isolation where the Enemies of Excellence will eliminate him.

In my years of experience in working with leaders, *it's always their isolation that ultimately leads to their fall*, as we will explore in more detail in the next two chapters. This is a truth that every expert in war strategy knows: if you're isolated, you're an easy target to take out. The opposite is also true: if you're connected in caring relationships, you are strong and very difficult to destroy.

We Need Each Other

Humans do better when they are connected in caring relationships with other humans. This sounds so simplistic, almost elementary, but in today's fast-paced world, it's revolutionary. We have more devices and ways to connect than ever before in the history of mankind, and yet we are isolated. We have smart phones and can Facebook, tweet, or e-mail 24 hours a day, but does that really build authentic connection? These devices can enhance our connection as we share our lives, they cannot connect our hearts or emotions like shared experiences.

We need to do life together! We need to be face-to-face, speaking into each other's lives, helping each other and sharpening each other. We need to love and be loved by a select group of people. I recently finished the Hood-to-Coast Relay. I spent 24 hours in a van with 6 other sweaty, smelly guys who each did his best in running one leg of the relay. One guy would run while the rest of us drove next to him and cheered him on. We worked with our other team, a van of six runners, to leapfrog our way 197 miles from Mt. Hood to seaside Oregon, where we finished with thousands of other crazy people. We loved it! We ran, shared, ate, slept, and bonded in relationship at a level you could never achieve on Facebook.

What alarms me with so many of the leaders I meet is that they don't have critical connections with key people in their life. They don't have people in their van. They're trying to do the race of life all on their own, without any support. They are living life and doing leadership without any safety net.

When you are running hard, who is there to cheer you? When you run out of water, who is there to help you rehydrate and keep going to the finish line?

At a more intimate level, who knows your thoughts, motives, weaknesses, challenges, and opportunities? Who are you doing life with? What I have seen in the leaders I've coached is that those who have connected, caring relationships with a good level of intimacy are stronger, more successful, and stable than those who don't.

What I observed in these stronger, successful leaders is that they had five Critical Connections that provided them stability and a network of trusted advisors who together defeated all the Enemies of Excellence, especially the Enemy of Broken Relationships.

Most people have the four Critical Connections that you see in Diagram 1, below. What I found fascinating was that successful leaders

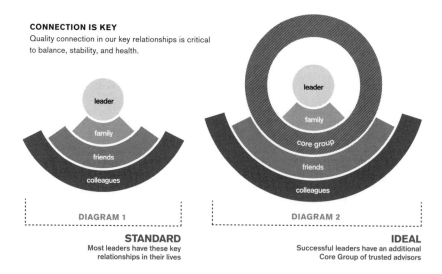

critical connections

CONNECTION IS KEY
Quality connection in our key relationships is critical to balance, stability, and health.

leader
family
friends
colleagues

DIAGRAM 1

STANDARD
Most leaders have these key relationships in their lives

leader
family
core group
friends
colleagues

DIAGRAM 2

IDEAL
Successful leaders have an additional Core Group of trusted advisors

have an additional Core Group of people in their Critical Connections, as you can see in Diagram 2.

The Core Group had three to five members; they provided a higher level of friendship and freely spoke about motives, behaviors, and actions. They were there to brainstorm and help provide insight into leadership challenges, business dealings, financial issues, dating, marriage, and parenting, as well as extended family challenges. When crisis struck, as it inevitably does in life, they would console as the person in pain recovered. The Core Group mutually cared for each other. The relationships were reciprocal with other members. The Core Group did not own each other's life, they enhanced it. The goal was to equip and empower each member, not control them. People in the Core Group had a greater sense of well-being, worth, and stability. They were more creative and approached life with more confidence and faith.

It was interesting that the Core Group sometimes shifted, with some members moving out and new members moving in, but the successful leaders always ensured they had a Core Group. They understood that you don't do life without it. It's very dangerous and a huge mistake to be disconnected from people who will encourage as well as correct you when needed.

Building Your Critical Connections

Now is the time to enhance or build your Critical Connections. Who's in your circles of key relationships? Who are the people in your Core Group? In this next exercise, you will consider who should be in each of your circles of Critical Connections and build your Core Group. Grab your calendar and consider how you might increase your connection in all your circles. Once you select the names of key people in your Core Group, I encourage you to contact them and get together. Discuss what roles you would like the Core Group members to play in each other's lives. Discuss how often you would like to connect and how you can care for each other.

Up Next

By using the tools in this chapter, you've enhanced your ability to recognize where you are most likely to indulge in destructive excess. By building a Core Group, you've also strengthened your ability to get support from people who support your success. Relationships matter. Life was not designed to be lived alone. Yet many people still isolate themselves. Why? Let's explore why leaders drive from their lives the key people who care about them the most. The answers will surprise you.

Chapter Eight

The Enemy of Isolation

This chapter will equip you to:

- Understand why people isolate themselves.
- Increase your EQ (emotional intelligence).
- Build accountability into your life for greater sustainability.

It's September 1938, and Europe is teetering on the brink of another world war. Peace in the wake of "The War to End All Wars" proved to be just a mirage. From the ashes of a devastated Germany rose Adolf Hitler. His eyes were fixed on a prime piece of real estate for his empire—the Sudetenland, a prized border region belonging to Czechoslovakia. The German nationalists rallied to Hitler's cause, hungry for political empowerment in their marginalized position.[1] The Munich Agreement set into motion a perfect storm, as a counsel of world leaders placated the demands of the Führer.

Just six months later, the world looked at the German occupation of Czechoslovakia as confirmation of the inevitable—there would be war. "My patience is now at an end," said Hitler in a Berlin speech delivered September 26, 1938, shortly before the signing of the Munich Treaty.[2] While playing the charade of protecting the Sudeten German minority from the Czech majority, Hitler positioned his military machinery for a full-scale invasion of Europe. Hitler's rhetoric of peace and his charismatic persona, which fooled even world leaders such as British Prime minister Neville Chamberlain, disguised his hunger for total domination.

What is particularly fascinating about Hitler's diabolical plans is that they were always out in the open. His leadership of the German National Socialist (Nazi) Party in 1920 signaled trouble from the start. When in jail in 1923, he revealed his entire tyrannical plan, penned in his autobiography *Mein Kampf,* in which he promised the seizure of lands Germany had lost in World War I. This would be achieved by uniting all Germans under a single reign of domination in Eastern Europe—the "thousand year Reich."[3] Few questioned his sanity or attempted to hold him accountable until it was too late.

Six million Jews slaughtered. Countless lives lost on the battlefield. We wonder how someone like Hitler could have achieved such destruction. An ancient proverb shines light on this critical subject. *"Whoever isolates himself seeks his own desire; he breaks out against all sound judgment."* (Proverbs 18:1) Whether it's in ancient Israel or our world today, the Enemy of Isolation finds his way into the minds and hearts of talented leaders.

The Insanity of Isolation

The Enemy of Isolation is a powerful predator. He deals in destruction. His plan of attack is to divide and conquer. He wants us to leave the presence of others and go it alone, to be the maverick who ends up masterminding his own demise.

Anyone who is not held to accountability is a danger to himself, the people he leads, and the organization he represents. The more isolated a leader is, the more insulated he becomes from outside insight. He becomes locked in his own sense of idealism, one that inevitably lacks enough realism. His view of himself and the world is askew. He forms ideas and makes decisions independent of input from other team members and misses out on their insight. Often, he then demands that his ideas be implemented *immediately*, rather than after others have had a chance to examine them. An isolated leader is so blinded by his outrageous ambition that he battles with anyone who dares to stand in his way.

Why do we, like Neville Chamberlain, allow appeasement? To appease is to yield to the hostile demands of someone else, not because it's the right thing to do, but because we hope to gain some form of peace. Unfortunately, it never works, and worse, someone somewhere always gets hurt. Countless individuals throughout history have suffered because someone refused to hold someone else accountable.

When you face a situation that affects someone else, it is not a time to cower. It's a time to exercise courage and confront. You might hesitate because you feel you're demeaning or interfering with someone else's leadership, but in fact you're giving him precisely what he needs to be successful and avoid danger. An isolated leader desperately needs to be brought into accountability, just as each of us needs to be accountable to someone in order to avoid our own isolation. To appease a leader is to abandon him to deploy his talents in destructive rather than constructive pursuits.

A detached leader is dangerous because, as we saw earlier, he's an egotist who believes he is smarter than most people. In fact, one of the most consistent red flags I've seen in my coaching is when I hear a leader tell me "most people consider me to be smart." Why do so many leaders feel the need to tell me this, and tell me this in the first ten minutes? Of course, some people are considered to be smart, but when I hear this, I know that the person has low social awareness and a need to impress me. He's trying to control the perception of the person he's talking to. This is classic Isolation behavior.

The Aim of Accountability

Rob was failing. Even his need to succeed at all costs was waning. Rob had allowed the Enemies of Excellence to push him further and further into isolation. He was doing his best to preserve his highly polished public persona, but he was just so tired. He was tired of the secret sins, the long lonely hours, and the lack of peace. He was an independent operator outside of any oversight. He reported to a directing board, but he refused to make use of their governance.

Lacking the protective covering of accountability, he wandered aimlessly. This is no surprise: accountability is a sentry against self-sabotage. Like Rob, we might think that it will constrict us, but it doesn't limit us—it frees us to fly higher. When we allow the right people to examine our motives, decisions, and actions, we excel. They warn us if are walking in the wrong direction and help us make better decisions. They help us achieve more with greater results. In other words, accountability allows us to be our best. It's not a hindrance but a helping hand.

Accountability works best when it's invited. We need to invite the right people into our lives and grant them permission to review who we are and how we live. When we choose our own accountability partners, we gain people we can trust, and that trust leads to greater vulnerability. To be vulnerable is to be open to correction and criticism. Vulnerability allows ethical, moral, social, and intellectual dialogue to discover greater truth. Vulnerability protects us from being susceptible to harmful decisions and directions in our life and leadership.

EQ

Accountability also provides a unique opportunity to advance our emotional intelligence (EQ). EQ is critical to your success. When EQ was first discovered, it served to explain something that had puzzled scientists. When you compare the performance levels of people with different intelligence quotients (IQs), people with the highest IQs outperformed those with average IQs 20 percent of the time, while people with average IQs outperformed those with higher IQs 70 percent of the time. Scientists realized there must be another variable besides IQ that could explain success. Years of research pointed to emotional intelligence (EQ) as the critical factor.[4]

What was observed in the study is demonstrated in real-life situations as well. If emotional intelligence is so critical to our success, what is it and how do we build it? EQ is your ability to recognize and understand emotions in yourself and others, and your ability to use this awareness to manage your behavior and relationships. It affects how you navigate social complexities and make personal decisions that achieve positive results.[5]

EQ is made up of four primary skills. The first two, self-awareness and self-management, are primarily about you. The second two, social awareness and relationship management, are more about how you are with other people.[6] When you examine the four EQ skills, it becomes easy to understand why people with average intelligence can outperform people with high intelligence. In my view, EQ is the IQ multiplier that maximizes our ability to succeed in life and leadership.

What happens when you isolate yourself? You lose your ability to interact well with other people, and your self-awareness decreases rapidly. When, however, you reject isolation and determine to live life with a Core Group of trusted advisors, your ability to recognize and make good use of emotions increases—in other words, you EQ soars. And this does not take place in a theoretical vacuum. It's in the regular interactions between people that your transformation and growth take place.

Making Accountability Count

Consider the safety and sustainable success that accountability can secure. It's like a bulletproof vest to protect your vital organs. When the Enemies of Excellence take a shot at you, they will not penetrate your heart. With some self-disclosure in your Core Group, you'll discover how to defeat not only the Enemy of Isolation but also the Enemies of Egotism, Life Mismanagement, Bad Habits, Indulgence, and Broken Relationships.

For self-disclosure and accountability to work, however, you need to avoid generalities and vague words. Be sure to provide your Core Group members with specific areas of focus. Where do you most need responsible, caring people to assist your success? What areas of your personal and professional life need focused accountability? While completing the exercise below, consider the following categories to build your Accountability Tracker. An Accountability Tracker

Accountability Tracker

The Accountability Tracker has five areas of focus.

1. **Accountability Accounts**: You will see seven sample Accountability Accounts for you to consider. You are welcome to add or subtract accounts.
2. **Focus Items**: The Focus Items are your list of personal and professional subjects you want to focus on within each Accountability Account.
3. **Action Items**: These are Action Steps you will take on a regular basis to address the Focus Items in your Accountability Accounts.
4. **Personal Updates**: Personal Updates are the tools you use to track your progress in each Accountability Account.
5. **Core Group Updates**: This section allows you to record your Core Group's encouragement and their evaluation of your Accountability Account progress.

ACCOUNT- ABILITY ACCOUNTS	FOCUS ITEMS	ACTION ITEMS	PERSONAL UPDATES	CORE GROUP UPDATES
Ethics				
Morals				
Emotions				
Relationships				
Money				
Recreation				
Thoughts				

ensures that you will disclose everything you want to disclose and equips the members of your Core Group to assist you in your success. There is a digital version of the Accountability Tracker available at *www.coachgreg.com* under "Tools."

Up Next

Building on the idea of a Core Group, this chapter has shown the dangers of isolation and the importance of people to whom you can be accountable in your life and work. Stories like Rob's remind us of the dire consequences of isolating ourselves from those who can hold us accountable and enrich our success.

Have you ever wondered why talented, intelligent leaders don't turn their lives around before they totally destroy themselves through Isolation? Surely, we think, they must know that they are living on the edge and are about to fall. What prevents them from saving themselves? In the next chapter, you will learn the answer to that question and discover how to avoid self-sabotage in your own life.

Chapter Nine

The Enemy of Self-Sabotage

This chapter will equip you to:

- Recognize the most dangerous leadership traps.
- Establish safeguards against self-sabotage.
- Build a weekly schedule that protects your personal and professional priorities.

The Darkness of Deception

His chilling confession rocked the Evangelical world. In his November 5, 2006 farewell letter to his former 14,000-member church, Ted Haggard described his demise by saying:

> "I am a deceiver and a liar. There is a part of my life that is so repulsive and dark that I've been warring against all of my adult life. For extended periods of time, I would enjoy victory and rejoice in freedom. Then from time to time, the dirt that I thought was gone would resurface, and I would find myself thinking thoughts and experiencing desires that were contrary to everything I believe and teach."

This is a sad and sobering confession of betrayal.[1] In the public eye, Haggard had been at the pinnacle of success. He was the president of National Association of Evangelicals. He had access to the White House and was consulted frequently by the president and members of Congress. He led one of the largest churches in America, one that he and his wife Gayle had started in the basement of their home 20 years earlier. So his admission of adultery was both a betrayal of his congregation and a betrayal of the very person who had worked by his side year after year. In his public life, Haggard appeared to be perfect. It was his private life that proved to be the source of his despair and demise.

The Gap

There was a dangerous gap between Ted's public image and his private world. Ted left open a door that allowed the Enemy of Self-Sabotage to enter and get to work. This final Enemy is like a serpent, slithering silently behind the other Enemies of Excellence and setting the trap of self-deception. Once a person is caught in this trap, The Enemy of Self-Sabotage leaves and lets the leader experience the fallout.

Leaders deceive themselves in many ways. In my experience, here are a few of the self-deception traps that lead to self-sabotage.

- The self-deception of many leaders begins with the Enemy of Egotism. A leader believes "I really know what is best for me, my team, and this organization." Notice I say that he believes it, not that it is true. He truly believes that he has special insights and talents that don't require anyone else's input and balance. The gap between his personal life and public persona widens because this leader is isolated and doesn't allow other people to speak into his life. The higher the egotism, the lower the emotional intelligence. This means that the egocentric leader keeps undermining his leadership because his self-awareness and self-management are low. You will notice poor listening skills, outbursts of anger, and immature behavior, all of which contribute to self-sabotage.

- Many leaders who are susceptible to the Enemy of Self-Sabotage have extraordinary personalities. They are usually physically attractive and emotionally engaging, and they use these abilities to their advantage. This combination of charisma and other gifts can skyrocket them to success. Yet herein lies the problem. Most leaders who enjoy rapid success experience a serious gap. Because success has come so quickly, and character is slower to develop than talents and abilities, their character is inevitably less developed than their talents. Yet, like all of us, they need character to sustain success. Aggravating the problem is that the more successful they are, the less likely they are to recognize the gap, even if others try to point it out to them. They reason, "I'm enjoying success, so what's the problem?" The problem, of course, is that it's one thing to build success, and something else entirely to maintain it. *What got you there won't keep you there.* The other challenge to successful leaders is handling the applause. Of course, they usually can't. Who can? Think about this for a moment. No one taught us to handle applause. You don't think about it because you never imagined yourself getting applause. And then it happens. The leader thinks, "Hey I could get used to this!" Pretty soon, he has to have it, and he will do anything to get it, including surrounding himself with people who silently applaud him. His life is gone.[2]
- Another level of self-deception is the ability to postpone doing what the leader knows he has to do to fix the situation. He thinks, "I'll get around to it," a dangerous idea that invites the Enemy of Life Mismanagement. Countless leaders think they are climbing the summit of success when they are actually digging a deep pit, one they never escape from. Once they start to mismanage personal priorities, they create big gaps in their own health and

key relationships. Are you seeing more clearly how the Enemies of Excellence work?

- The Enemy of Life Mismanagement hands off to the Enemy of Bad Habits. A leader in emergency mode is just trying to put out fires in his personal life. He is too tired to do things right and well, so he tries just to "get it done." This approach inevitably can't solve problems, breeds more Bad Habits, and merely fuels the leader's failure.

- Unless the gap is closed with the Enemies of Egotism, Life Mismanagement, and Bad Habits, a leader sinks into deeper despair. The Enemy of Indulgence for most leaders is an escape. Unable to make sense of the gap that now exists between his personal and public face, a leader turns to indulgent behavior to buffer the problems building around him. Have you ever seen footage of a tornado that seems to blow in from nowhere and strike with severe force? Just so, the final three Enemies of Broken Relationships, Isolation, and Self-Sabotage appear. Their self-deception disorientates the leader. He is so stripped of his bearings, he literally doesn't know where to turn, so he runs with no direction and no one to help him. Another one bites the dust.

In the final days of Rob's self-sabotage, it was painful to witness his fall. He would never again enjoy the level of success he had possessed. Everything he had worked for was falling apart. He was drenched in scandal. His board and staff no longer backed him. Once dedicated to his vision, people now saw him as a villain. His marriage, family, health, finances, and friendships were fractured and in desperate need of help. Once a man of courage and strength, he now appeared to be fearful and fragile. He didn't know which way to turn because he was dizzy with self-destruction.

It's a desperate state to be in. If you've used some of the tools in this book and begun your work early enough, you've learned to defeat the Enemies so that your life won't deteriorate to this point. If not, you know too well what it's like to experience this self-sabotage. You're disoriented, discouraged, and depressed all at the same time.

Is there a way out?

Closing the Gap

There is a way out. It begins with the only antidote for the lies we tell ourselves. We need the truth. It's the only thing that will expose the lies of the Enemies of Excellence, contend with self-destruction, and set our feet on solid ground. Only the truth will set us free.

We need to step away from the frenzied fray of life and leadership to discover the truth about our head, heart, and habits.

How is your head? Have you been able to clear the confusion in your mind and discover the truth about your life and leadership? Once you can see and understand your current state of affairs, you can move towards greater success. The exercises in each chapter in this book have been designed to lead you to better understanding. If you're clear, then proceed. If you still have some questions regarding some of the Enemies of Excellence, I recommend that you return to those chapters. Read them again and run through the exercises one more time to see if clarity emerges. Consider including a friend or trusted advisor to engage in dialogue with you regarding the subject of your concern. Dialogue combined with active listening is a wonderful way to increase insight and understanding.

How is your heart? Are you establishing the right priorities for gaining greater spiritual, emotional, relational, and physical health? I want to encourage you to pull back from work and place more focus on your personal life. I coach so many people who are waiting to live their lives. They're waiting until work gets "less busy" or the kids go to college or they retire. The sobering reality is that you don't know how long you have to live. You may not even have tomorrow. Imagine the thousands of people on September 11, 2001, who thought they were just going to work that day. They had no idea that day would be their last. Do you think when they faced the moment that their lives were about to be over, they were concerned about e-mail and the projects on their desk? They were focused entirely on whether they would live, and the people they loved. They saw the important things of life more clearly than you and I see them right now. They understood how precious life is. If your life was coming to an end today would you have regrets? What would they be? Please consider my encouragement as a permission slip to place a higher importance upon your life. Your work is an important part of your life, but if it has become your life, you need to change your priorities.

How are your habits? Do your daily efforts reflect your priorities? Here is a truth I share with the people I coach: what you do each day is a reflection of your week, your month, your year. What you do in an average day is really a reflection of your life.

You can test this claim for yourself. In this last exercise, which you can find at *www.coachgreg.com* under "Tools," design your Ideal Week. An Ideal Week reflects the ideal of how you want to live and lead. It contains within it both your personal and professional priorities. Begin now to build your Ideal Week, and create a place for every major area of your life. Make each priority an appointment that you will keep. Build your Ideal Week into your calendar and begin practicing and refining it for the next 30 days. Not only will it improve your habits—it will improve your heart and your head.

Up Next

With the Ideal Week exercise and the others you've completed to this point, you're better equipped to be the effective leader you are called to be. You've encountered some of the thoughts and words that leaders use when they begin to sabotage their own lives, and you've been able to assess your own life in light of those dangerous attitudes. With this knowledge of the 7 Enemies of Excellence, you're ready to take the next step and begin fulfilling your life's purpose. In the next chapter, let's look at several ways to understand your purpose—how to identify it and put it into practice.

Chapter Ten

Experiencing Excellence

"Most men lead lives of quiet desperation."

Many people, especially those with an interest in management and spiritual growth, have seen this famous quote from Henry David Thoreau. It's often used to point to the struggle many people have in finding meaning and value in life. When you hear this quote, the implied message is usually, "You don't want to become one of those people." But what can you do to avoid desperation? What step can you take? Thoreau himself gives us a ray of light, and it's a shame that people so rarely remember the full quotation in all its wisdom. *"Most men lead lives of quiet desperation and go to the grave with the song still in them."*

Bull's eye! What a perfect summary of our human condition. Thoreau wrote as he witnessed life unfolding. He looked around him and saw people living each day as mere survivors, never quite rising above the level of subsistence. He saw a sea of people trudging through life, never realizing their purpose, and passing away with their song or passion still locked inside their heart. I see this same thing today. Don't you?

Pursuing Your Purpose

It takes courage to pursue your purpose and sing your own passionate song. After all, some people specialize in silencing other people's songs. They surely don't want you to discover yours. They abhor people who passionately sing their song, for it represents a life they don't know. The purpose of their life is anti-purpose: they want to prove that life is somber, without music—you endure life, and then you end it. That's it! Of course, they could not be more wrong. We all are endowed with a song to sing, one that gives us joy and brings music to our world.

If you wait around for people like that to give you the approval to sing, you too will go to the grave with a song unsung. It's time for you to write your own permission slip and passionately pursue your purpose. Discover what other leaders have discovered: you can live today with greater purpose and passion. You can remove the lid that limits you, build a better life, and be a better leader. Your can conquer the Enemies of Excellence. It's time to forge forward and experience excellence.

Identifying Your Purpose

In this book, unlike in many other books of the kind, I have not attempted to define excellence but rather what is sabotaging it. In my experience, most people know what it would mean for them to succeed and achieve excellence in their lives, both in small matters and large. Purpose, however, is a different matter. What is your life's purpose? How do you find what song you are meant to sing?

There is an ancient proverb that discusses the importance of bringing to the surface the insights in our hearts. Proverbs 20:5 says: "The purpose in a man's heart is like deep water, but a man of understanding will draw it out."

Here is a powerful exercise for "drawing out" the purpose in your heart. As we approach the end of the journey we are taking in this book, I want you to think about the end of the journey you will take in life. Imagine that you are at the end of your life, looking back. What would you want people to say about you as they gather around you? As you think through this exercise, you'll discover that your purpose is more obvious than you think. It comes out in what you most naturally enjoy doing. It doesn't drain you but fills you up and fuels your passion. And it can be seen in a few simple clarifying questions. So I want you to do a short exercise to imagine what you would like people to say about your life. But I want you to do this not just for your life as it is, but your life as you'd like it to be. In other words, don't simply think about how people would talk about you today, but how they would talk about the "you" you want to become once you fulfill your life's purpose.

When we give ourselves time to stop and think, the important matters in our heart can be mined and brought to the surface. Our purpose in life can emerge, and we can pursue life fueled with passion.

Clarifying Questions

- What are your greatest strengths?
- What do others say you "do very well"?
- What do people say you "should be doing with your life"? Examples: "You're so good at mentoring, you should train employees." "You take care of details so well, I wish we could give you all of our data."
- What activities do you enjoy doing the most?
- If you could dedicate your life to accomplishing just one thing, what would it be?
- If you could describe your purpose in one sentence what would you say?

My purpose in life is to:

_____

_____

_____

Passion follows purpose and is what makes us fully alive. Then, when we wake up each day with purpose and passion, we have energy to pursue our full potential. We can push through the barriers that block us from building and experiencing excellence.

Practicing Your Purpose

To realize your purpose, you need to identify it. Then you need to practice it. I encourage you to discover ways that you can structure your life more around what you love to do. In your life and work, restructure what you do each day to have greater connection with your purpose. You don't necessarily need to change your profession to engage more fully in your purpose. But you will most likely need to change *how you do your work*. With a little innovation and interaction with the people you work with, you can redesign your days to engage your purpose and be more productive.

Let's consider the example of Susan, who has always known that she has a passion to expand her own knowledge and to teach others as well. If she restructured her work, how would it change?

1. *Mondays and Wednesdays*: mentor a local student who does not know how to read well.
2. *Tuesdays and Thursdays*: invest time preparing for a certification test for her field.
3. *Fridays*: meet with a local colleague who has experience in her field and has offered to mentor her.

What action steps would she need to take this week to make these changes a reality in her life?

1. Stop working through her lunch hour. (Her company has never asked her to do this, so this requires no special permission.)
2. Ask her supervisor if she can take an extra 30 minutes at lunch and make it up by staying 30 minutes later in the day.

3. Notify her business associates in-house and throughout the industry so that they know she is away from her desk at that time.

This may seem like a small example, but I'll give you two pieces of insight. First, these 90 minutes a day add up very quickly and can transform your life and the lives of others. Second, I've never met an employee who was told "no" when they asked for this kind of arrangement.

Now apply this same exercise to your own life. If you restructured your work to reflect your purpose, what would change? Consider the desired changes you have written down. Which are you ready to act upon? Place a check mark by the items you are now ready to change now. Finally, determine the action steps you need to take this week to make these changes a reality.

Many times, it's the simple things that can create enormous change. Small changes can transform lives. They work for leaders who need only small adjustments in their work as well as leaders who have completely fallen apart. In fact, they even worked for Rob.

My Final Meeting with Rob

It had been 3 years since Rob's catastrophic collapse. Rob's traumatic experience helped me clarify and identify so many of the patterns I had witnessed in other high-profile leaders, and throughout our coaching meetings together, I had done my best to offer him the same guidance I've offered you throughout this book. I couldn't help but wonder—had he made a turnaround? Had the coaching been worth it?

I decided to contact him. He agreed to meet while I was traveling in his area. As I drove to the restaurant, I wondered how things in his life had changed. How were his marriage and family? How was he recovering from his failure? Had he managed to rebuild his home life?

My mind was racing as I pulled into the parking lot. Rob and I had been friends for more than a decade, and my hope was that he had discovered how to turn his life around.

I saw him pull in and wave to me. I went to his car, and we greeted each other. It was good to see him but a bit awkward for both of us as well. We went into the restaurant and grabbed a booth where we would not be disturbed. We sat down and exchanged small talk about sports and how our favorite teams were doing. Being athletes, we instantly connected at this common interest level.

I began to ask some questions.

"How's your family?"

"They're really doing well," he answered. "We had the kids in an academy but decided to have them home for a time to homeschool them. This allows us to travel with them and enjoy fun experiences together."

Wow! He seemed more focused on family than I'd ever seen him. I could see genuine excitement as he described the latest fishing trip with his boys, who saw their Dad catch a 200-pound sturgeon. Rob needed two other men to help him pull the beast to shore. Rob's oldest son was able to sit on the monster before they let it return to the deep regions of the river. This was encouraging. Rob was turning his personal life around. Rob had always been a deeply driven man, primarily focused on his work, but now I could see he was also driven to have a connected, caring family.

"How's your marriage?" I asked

"Well, we're in counseling," he said. "I'm beginning to learn the triggers that kick off conflict. The counselor forces disclosure and mines for confrontation to bring key issues out in the open. To use an analogy, we've moved from being in intensive care to physical therapy, and we're working on growing our relationship."

"That's encouraging, Rob," I affirmed. "It must feel much better to be at this place than three years ago."

"Yes!" he said. "It's a new beginning. We're learning a lot."

"How's work?" I asked.

"My work is going really well. I'm a top salesman, and the income is great. The funds are allowing us to take special trips with the kids; in fact we leave tomorrow on another trip. I'm a highly trusted team member and enjoy the people at work. I've actually begun to mentor some people."

I listened as Rob shared the details of how he was reinventing his life. I was glad that he'd thrown himself into restoring and reestablishing the important priorities for a healthy life. He was defeating the Enemies of Excellence. His house was not going to be rebuilt overnight, and he clearly understood that. But by finding his purpose and understanding how important it was for him to be a good father, husband, and role model, he had stopped sabotaging himself and was building a strong foundation for success to last in the long run.

Excellence in Your Sights

In this book, I've shown you that leadership is intrinsically dangerous—to be a leader, whether in politics, business, education, ministry, or the home, means that you will face certain kinds of temptations. There is simply no way to avoid them. But this is not the end of the story. Take a look at the cover of this book. You see that "excellence" is the crosshairs of a rifle sight. I hope I've convinced you that The Enemies of Excellence are out to destroy you, trying to weaken your resolve so that your own life, and the lives of those who rely on you, are damaged. But imagine disarming The Enemies of Excellence, day by day, exercise by exercise, so that the sight is now a viewing glass. You can see your excellence much more clearly than before. It's magnified, and you see it in all its color and detail.

The Enemies of Excellence can be overcome, and they must overcome. You need to succeed, but in fact, we all need you to succeed. Every time a leader fails, we all suffer, because our ability to trust people in a necessary role is weakened. The world cannot function without effective leaders, and we need more of them. *The Enemies of*

Excellence is designed to be a road-map to help you succeed. Invest the energy and time you need to break through the leadership behaviors that sabotage your success. Make use of the tools in this book, and refer to the *Next Steps* section at the end of this book to learn about additional materials we offer you online at *www.coachgreg.com*.

And finally, if you find that you want additional support, remember that there is a team of passionate professionals waiting to serve you. We specialize in coaching, team training, and consulting, so that every one of us can be an example of excellence to better our world!

Greg Salciccioli
Professional Leadership Coach
www.coachgreg.com

Next Steps

The following resources, training, and coaching opportunities are offered to assist your personal and professional development. To learn more and preview the resources and services featured below please visit www.coachgreg.com

VALUABLE RESOURCES

The Enemies of Excellence Growth Guide provides leaders, managers, and facilitators a practical tool to implement the valuable lessons in The Enemies of Excellence. The Growth Guide is designed for your personal and team growth. It will assist you and the people you lead in overcoming the Enemies of Excellence to achieve greater personal and professional excellence.

The Growth Guide works with The Enemies of Excellence material and contains additional lessons, tools and best practices. It is a valuable tool to maximize learning and raise your level of leadership, as well as that of your team members, and the organization you lead. To preview this resource please visit www.coachgreg.com.

TOOLS

The Enemies of Excellence "Tools" are free downloads at www.coachgreg.com to assist your learning and collaboration with others as you read and apply the lessons in The Enemies of Excellence book and Growth Guide.

TRAINING OPPORTUNITY

The *Excellence Event* is a one-day event led by Coach Greg Salciccioli at your location. It focuses on eliminating The Enemies of Excellence and building a Personal Excellence Plan as well as leadership best practices to increase staff engagement and productivity.

This event includes additional training and resources not contained in The Enemies of Excellence book or Growth Guide. This event is highly effective in raising the level of personal and professional excellence in your staff and organization. To learn more about how the *Excellence Event* can benefit your team, staff or organization please visit www.coachgreg.com and select "Speaking" to learn more and have an event representative contact you.

COACHING OPPORTUNITY

Coaching is a powerful growth process that is proven to get results. A professional coach bridges the gap between where you are to where you want to be. Your Coach provides valuable insight as a trusted advisor resulting in clearer direction and greater achievement. To learn more, please visit www.coachgreg.com and select "Coaching" to discover how professional coaching works and to have a coaching representative contact you.

the
enemies
of
excellence

greg salciccioli

The Growth Guide *is designed for your personal growth*

Notes

Chapter 1

1. Goodall, Wayde. *Why Great Men Fall: 15 Winning Strategies to Rise Above it All*. (Green Forest: New Leaf Press, 2005), 13.

Chapter 2

1. Garver, Eugene. Introduction and Notes. *Poetics and Rhetoric* (New York: Barnes and Noble, 2005) 35.

Chapter 3

1. Murdoch, Lachlan. Foreword. In Lincoln Hall, *Dead Lucky: Life after Death on Mt. Everest* (New York: Penguin, 2007).
2. Cowell, Alan. "'Dead' Climber's Survival Impugns Mount Everest Ethics." *NYTimes.com*, 28 May 2006. Web. 19 Jan. 2010.
3. "Everest Climbers Recall Near-death Experience." *MSNBC.com*. NBC News and News Services. 12 June, 2006. Web. 19 Jan, 2010.
4. "Miracle on Mount Everest." *Dateline NBC*. Nar. Matt Lauer. 27 May 2008. Web 20 Jan. 2010. Transcript.
5. "Everest Climbers Recall Near-death Experience."
6. Cowell, op. cit.
7. Cowell, op. cit.
8. Benoist, Michael. "Ask Adventure: Everest Cents." National Geographic Adventure Magazine. *National Geographic Society*. May 2003. Web. 31 Jan 2010.
9. *Good to Great* (New York: Harper Collins, 2001) 21.
10. Creswell, Julie and Landon Thomas Jr. "The Talented Mr. Madoff." *NYTimes.com*. New York Times. 25 Jan. 2009. Web. 9 Nov. 2009.

Chapter 8

1. *Czechoslovakia: A Country Study*. Ed. Ihor Gawdiak. Washington: GPO for the Library of Congress, 1987. N. pag. *Country Studies US*. Web. 8 Feb. 2010.
2. *Speeches that Changed the World*, 78.
3. *Speeches that Changed the World, 80*.
4. Travis Bradberry and Jean Greaves, "Emotional Intelligence 2.0. Henceforth "EI".
5. "EQ"
6. "EQ"

Chapter 9

1. Lee Sparks, "Public Perfection Private Despair," Jan/Feb 2007 rev.org.
2. Lee Sparks, "Public Perfection Private Despair," Jan/Feb 2007 rev.org.

Crossroad Books for Your Leadership Library

For leaders of all kinds, Crossroad offers books to help you move to a deeper level. Here is just a few of our books you should know about.

If you have ever wondered if there is a better way to decide how to spend your money and whom to donate to, this next book is essential reading. In *What Your Money Means: And How to Use It Well,* Frank J. Hanna challenges us to think about our money in a different way. If we are honest, even in these difficult financial times many of us have more than we need for mere survival. The chapters of this book lead us to identify what our essential needs are and how best to use the money that is not essential.

If you have had enough experience as the leader of a group to witness both the successes and downturns of an organization, you will benefit from *The Soul of a Leader: Finding Your Path to Success and Fulfillment.* Drawing from real-life stories, Margaret Benefiel identifies several of the key challenges that organizations face in times of transition. She suggests practical, specific steps for identifying and strengthening the mission statement, putting it in place, and most importantly, remaining creative and flexible when setbacks occurs.

Staying true to your mission is also the central theme in Dave Durand's *Win the World Without Losing Your Soul.* This book takes on the idea that high levels of success can only come at the cost of personal integrity. Drawing from his own work consulting with organizations and seeing what works and doesn't work, Durand strengthens our ability to remain true to our convictions and true to our ambitions for success.

What Your Money Means: And How to Use It Well
978-0824525200

The Soul of a Leader: Finding Your Path to Success and Fulfillment
978-0824524807

Win the World without Losing Your Soul
978-0824526016

*Support your local bookstore or order
directly from the publisher by calling
1-800-888-4741 for customer service.*

*To request a catalog or inquire
about quantity orders, please e-mail
info@CrossroadPublishing.com.*

About the Author

Greg Salciccioli is an author, speaker, coach, and consultant. He has worked with hundreds of leaders to advance their excellence and organizational effectiveness.

He is a professional coach and the co-founder of Ministry Coaching International, a leadership coaching and consulting company that has helped thousands of ministry leaders worldwide.

His goal is to help leaders *be an example of excellence to better the world*. His inspirational approach and practical resources have proven to be highly effective in moving people forward in their life and leadership.

Greg lives in Oregon with his wife Dianna and their family. They enjoy the outdoors and spending time together.

To learn more about Coach Greg please visit www.coachgreg.com.